Living Healthy, Living Well

16 weeks of tips to begin a lifetime of healthy habits.

Substitutions, habits and inspirations. A common sense approach to obtaining and maintaining a healthy weight.

Shed pounds without deprivation, when you truly understand the energy value of food and exercise. A healthy mix of the two will have tremendous results.

A new approach to lose weight for life.

Phyllis Bullins, RN, CNT

Copyright © 2008 by Phyllis Bullins

All rights reserved. No part of this book shall be reproduced or transmitted in any form or by any means, electronic, mechanical, magnetic, photographic including photocopying, recording or by any information storage and retrieval system, without prior written permission of the publisher. No patent liability is assumed with respect to the use of the information contained herein. Although every precaution has been taken in the preparation of this book, the publisher and author assume no responsibility for errors or omissions. Neither is any liability assumed for damages resulting from the use of the information contained herein.

ISBN 0-7414-4912-9

Published by:

INFINITY
PUBLISHING.COM
1094 New DeHaven Street, Suite 100
West Conshohocken, PA 19428-2713
Info@buybooksontheweb.com
www.buybooksontheweb.com
Toll-free (877) BUY BOOK
Local Phone (610) 941-9999
Fax (610) 941-9959

Printed in the United States of America

Printed on Recycled Paper

Published August 2008

Table of Contents

My Story		1
Introduction		6
Week 1	Water, Water, and Water.	9
Week 2	Hunger, Satisfaction, Full, Empty?	15
Week 3	Move a Little More	21
Week 4	Do You Eat Breakfast???	25
Week 5	Variety is the Spice of Life	30
Week 6	Snacking	32
Week 7	Chose Healthy Grains	36
Week 8	Survival of the Weekend	39
Week 9	Tools of the Trade	41
Week 10	Get your Dairy Products	47
Week 11	Dining Out	48
Week 12	Social Hour and Parties	132
Week 13	Munching for Other than Hunger	134
Week 14	Goals	137
Week 15	Vacations and Holidays	138
Week 16	Maintenance	140
Nutrition 101		149

Favorite Recipes	151
Asparagus Omelet's	152
Broccoli Italian	154
Jell-O Salad	155
Italian Rice 'n Beans	156
Dreamy Creamy Potatoes	157
Baked Apple	158
Fish 'n Chips	159
Sour Cream Enchiladas	160
Chicken Tacos	161
Chicken 'n Artichokes	162
Fiesta Skillet Supper	163
Fall Day Beans	164
Watermelon Salad	165
Cream of Cauliflower Soup	166
Apple Crisp	167
Chicken Broccoli Stir-Fry	168
Cucumber and Sweet Pepper Salad	169
Orange Breakfast Cookie	170
Single serve Breakfast Bar	171
Greek Lentil Salad	172
Honey Stuffed Sweet Potatoes	173
Alfredo Style Noodles	174
Berry Chicken Salad	175
Grilled Sweet Potatoes	176
Apples with Ginger and Snow Peas	177
Toasted Angel Food Cake	178
Tips for Losing Weight	179
Budget Tips for Healthy Living	187

My Story

Many things define who we are in the world, throughout my life I have worn many faces. First of all, as an adult, I am a registered nurse. I have held many titles as a nurse. I began at the bedside, caring for patients. Then as an educator, teaching diet to chronically ill cardiac patients. I have also worked in administration and for several insurance companies. I have seen every aspect of ethics and live to tell about it. My second mask, as an adult is that of a wife and mother. With the birth of my second child I gained 80 pounds. Three of those after he was born, but before I left the hospital. How can that happen, it doesn't even make common sense. You deliver a six pound baby, eat nothing for 24 hours, go home in 2 days and weigh 3 pounds more that when you stepped on the scale at the labor admission.

Add to those baby pounds a stressful relocation, which was repeated several times with moves every 15 months. Each move packing on an additional 10 to 15 pounds a year, with the end journey yielding a very unhappy, unhealthy morbidly obese person. When the hole has been dug this deep, how in the world do you ever get out.

My professional career has evolved in my desire to make a real difference in your life. See, I found the way out, and I want to share it with you. I have done it. I have lost over 100 pounds and kept them off. Through a series of small, positive steps you can permanently get out of your ditch and never have a weight issue again. I have done it, made those small changes and found out how to succeed at the weight game.

Consult your personal physician before starting any weight-loss program. With making healthy food choices and increasing activity long term weight loss can be achieved. If you are taking medication, or following a therapeutic diet to treat a disease, please discuss this program with your physician before starting it.

Small steps yield big results.

First of all let me remind you that the weight you want to lose did not appear over night. If you are willing to make small changes for lasting results you will win at this game of weight loss for life.

Many diet plans and dieters insist on unreasonable unrealistic goals. They are accompanied by drastic lifestyle changes that can only be managed for a short time, and then old unhealthy habits return. My suggestion is that the changes are subtle and permanent and the goals are measurable, and attainable. With you having personal accountability and control over what the changes are.

To lose one pound a 3500 calorie deficit must be reached. The calories are energy for your body. When calories in do not equal calories out the result is weight gain. In return, when energy burned exceeds calories consumed the result is weight loss. It is a delicate balancing act. There are issues within our control and there are those that are not. Losing weight is not an easy task. It is not only difficult mentally, but physically it is very taxing and challenging. This is why my recommendation is to set a goal of not more that one pound per week. That is up to 52 pounds in a year.

You will incorporate simple eating and exercising changes into your busy schedule. These almost mindless changes will become habit and the weight loss will occur. This program is scientific, it is easy, and can be adapted to any lifestyle or appetite. Not only have I spent years studying and teaching nutrition. I personally have conquered the dinosaur. Won the race, I am not only out of the morbidly obese category, but I have a healthy Body Mass Index and I am healthier that any other time in my life. Losing weight required commitment and long term results require lifetime changes. When those changes are small, almost not noticed, they are easily adopted into a lifetime healthy habits. This is not a fanatical diet program. I love food. I always have and always will. This program takes away the rigid restrictions and frustration of deprivation with some programs. There is a tremendous health benefit to losing 10 percent of your body weight and maintaining a healthy Body Mass Index --BMI. You will hear a lot about the BMI or body mass index. It is a calculation using your height and weight that gives a healthy range for your weight. It is found by dividing your weight in Kilograms by your height in meters squared. It is used by medical professionals to determine overweight and obesity in adults. Overweight is defined with a BMI between 25 and 30, with obesity over 30. A healthy BMI for all adults is between 19 and less than 25. Health risks, such as adult diabetes, hypertension, arthritis, cardiovascular disease and some cancers increase with increasing BMI. The higher your BMI is over the healthy range, the more at risk you are for developing health problems.

Reaching a healthy weight and maintaining it is my goal for you. I did it and you can too.

This program does not restrict foods or require a commitment to the local gym. This plan encourages you to lose calories where you personally notice them the least, and therefore you will commit these changes to life. It also, adds activity in small steps as to not call for a complete lifestyle overhaul. The tortoise beats the hare with this program. It is not an all or nothing commitment, but one that is made part of positive lifestyle changes. The changes you will make will compliment your current lifestyle not restrict it. I have found the best way to use this book is read it through, then begin with week 1 and each week add a new tip to your weight loss plan. Small steps on a consistent basis, yields huge results.

Introduction

A Journal is very important and the first suggestion for success. Please take a moment and complete the questionnaire.

My weight is _____.

My Height is _____.

My current BMI is _____.

To have a Healthy BMI, my weight range should be _____.

My 10 percent weight loss goal is _____ pounds. I hope to achieve this goal weight loss by _____ (date) which is a total of _____ pounds (not to exceed 1.0) per week.

Congratulations!

The journey begins now.

So, are you ready to make a few changes? Begin with a one-week food diary. If you bite it, write it. This is a terrific tool for self-examination of your actual intake. Many times food is consumed without even being aware you are eating it. It is important that you become aware of what you eat, when you are eating, and why you are eating. A one-week journal of your behavior will probably be an eye opening experience. After the journal is complete, it will be easier to see where small changes can be made to save calories and lose pounds.

List the time of day, the food eaten, approximate calorie content (this means read the labels and watch portions), and lastly the degree of hunger. Use the scale of 1 being the hungriest you could imagine and 10 being so full, you feel stuffed. Also, as a reminder please total the fruits and vegetables, water and dairy products for the day.

In an effort to lose a pound a week, you must expend 500 more calories a day than you consume. Take a few minutes to look at the choices you are making, Are there places that you could decrease some hidden calories. Places like mayonnaise on your sandwich at lunch, or butter on the potato or bread. You may find it difficult to understand the value of a calorie at first, but it gets a lot easier and once you maneuver through the learning curve of educating yourself to what the calorie value is on the foods you are choosing, you will learn to budget those calories. The following 16 weeks will help you to be satisfied with the lower calorie choices you are making. Take one step at a time and enjoy the journey of becoming a healthier person. A calorie chart is listed at the end of the book to help you with some calorie choices. Labels are included on most foods you choose, begin reading those labels.

It is very important to make journaling your food choices your own, If your prefer to list your intake on the computer, do so. If you purchase a notebook and use that, Great. If you use a napkin before you eat that also works. Please put pen to paper. And before you eat anything, pause and think about what you are doing. Make certain you are in control and write down the food and the calories associated with the choice. So many members tell me this is the secret to their success and they have decided that maybe they do not want the choice once they really thought about it.

Find the system that means the most to you and commit to sixteen weeks of journaling your choice.

If you Bite it, write it....

Week ONE

Water, Water, and Water.

Water makes up most of your body. Many people walk around dehydrated on a daily basis and do not even realize it. The first small step suggestion is drinking more water.

On a routine day I drink _____ 8 ounce glasses of water. Please keep a journal for 7 days of the actual water you consume.

Day 1

Day 2

Day 3

Day 4

Day 5

Day 6

Day 7

When you actually tracked your water consumption were you surprised at the amount you were actually drinking? It is recommended that you drink 6 eight ounce glasses a day. Can you commit to increasing your water intake to reach this recommendation?

Tips to increase your water include drinking water with your meals. Serve your water in a beautiful glass. Add lemon or lime juice to jazz up the flavor. If you feel hungry between meals, start with a glass of water. Place a bottle of water by your bed and reach for it first thing in the morning. Have bottled water in the refrigerator in front of the calorie rich beverages. Many of us confuse hunger with thirst and trying a drink of water before a snack is a calorie saver.

By exchanging one 8 ounce glass of water for one 8 ounce serving of regular soda per day you have saved 100 calories per day or 3000 calories a month, 36,500 calories a year. This is equal to 10.4 pounds lost in one year. One little change consistently over a year yields a big loss.

If you do not routinely drink soda with calories, making the water change with a serving of juice would also have the same results.

20 Tips For Getting Your 6 Glasses of Water Daily

Sometimes drinking our six glasses of water a day can be a real challenge Here are 20 tips to help you accomplish that feat! It is said by many beauty experts that drinking your water is the cheapest, quickest way to look better! That sure motivates me!

1. Make a bet with a co-worker to see who can drink more water in the course of a day.

2. Have a big glass of water at every transitional point of the day: when you first get up, just before leaving the house, when you sit down to work, etc.

3. Make it convenient - keep a big, plastic, insulated water bottle full on your desk and reach for it all day.

4. When you have juice (apple, grape, or orange) fill half the glass with water.

5. When you have a junk-food craving, down a glass of water immediately. You feel full quickly and avoid the calories, and it lets time pass till the craving fades.

6. Have one glass every hour on the hour while at work. When the work day is done your water quota is met.

7. Substitute a cup of hot water with a drop of honey for tea or coffee.

8. While at work, get a 20 ounce cup of ice and keep filling it up from the office water cooler. The key is drinking with a straw - you take bigger gulps and

drink much more.

9. Freeze little bits of peeled lemons, limes, and oranges and use them in place of ice cubes - it's refreshing and helps get in a serving or two of fruit.

10. After each trip to the restroom, guzzle an eight-ounce glass to replenish your system.

11. Don't allow yourself a diet soda until you've had two to four glasses of water. You will find that you won't want the soda anymore or that just half a can is enough.

12. Let ounces of water double grams of fat: When eating something containing 10 grams of fat, I drink 20 ounces of water.

13. Drink two full glasses at each meal, one before and one after. Also, drink one glass before each snack so you don't eat as much.

14. Carry a small refillable water bottle at all times and drink during downtime; while waiting in a bank line, sitting on the train, etc.

15. Use a beautiful glass and fill it with cold water from the tap.

16. Drink two glasses of water immediately after waking up.

17. Bring a two-liter bottle of water to work and try to drink it all before you leave work. If you don't finish, drink it in traffic on the way home - it's like a race.

18. Always keep a 24-ounce bottle of water handy

while watching TV, doing laundry, making dinner, etc.

19. Add drinking two glasses of water to your daily skincare regimen. Drink, cleanse, moisturize, etc., then drink again.

20. Drink your water out of a big Pyrex measuring cup - it's a good way to keep track of how much water you are drinking.

This week remember to concentrate on getting 6 eight ounces glasses of water, tune into what hunger feels like and write down your food choices. You are well on your way to getting to your healthy self. Each week continue with the previous weeks tip and add to your healthy choices.

Below are examples of a food journal and can be duplicated into a note book, journal or computer. If you don't have it with you when you are about to munch on something. Pause for a second and write down what you are choosing on a napkin, Just the act of writing it down will give you the pause point to think about the choices you are making.

Time   Food   amount   calories   hunger

Water __ __ __ __ __ __

Dairy __ __ __

Fruits or veggies __ __ __ __ __

Week TWO

Hunger, satisfaction, full, empty?

Up to this point you have been eating as you normally would eat, and journaling the choices you make. By tracking where you put your calories and determining how many calories you take in on a daily basis you have determined how many calories is required to maintain your current weight. From this point forward you will decrease calories by 500 a day. We will look at ways to do this where you notice the deficit least. Continue to track the food you are eating and determine the calories on a daily basis. Does journaling your food feel like slavery or does it empower you to achieve the 500 calorie deficit.

Before you pick up your eating utensil, grab your pencil.

Now, that you have kept a journal for a week. You have a better idea of your choices and where some changes can be made. Take a few minutes and review the tips and ask your self-what changes you are willing to make to reach a healthy weight and Body Mass Index. There are three ways to lose weight. You can consume fewer calories, you can exert more energy by increasing your activity, or you can raise your resting metabolic rate through increasing muscle mass. A deficit of 250-500 calories a day will yield 1/2 to 1 pound of weight loss a week. Ask yourself what you are willing to do to improve your health. Can you increase your activity? Are you willing to lighten up your menu? Will you add more fruits and vegetables to your diet? Will you limit added sugars and alcohol? The following weeks have tips for making some small changes. They are to be used as a guideline to pick and choose from, with the ultimate goal of decreasing your daily calories by 500.

Also during this week, it is important to introduce your body to hunger. I know there were years that I did not have hunger. Many of us ignore the signal our stomach is sending our brain to the point that we no longer recognize why we should eat. I eat for two reasons. I eat for hunger and for pleasure. If I am eating for hunger, I constantly ask myself if I am satisfied. Through years of practice and consultation with many people who appear to have a handle on enough food being enough, I finally nailed where I was dropping the ball in the hunger signals. Several years ago I was having a celebration meal with a group of teenagers and college kids and my elementary age son. We had ordered several appetizer and they had been brought to the table and everyone was having a great time. Then I realized that the other people at the table had stopped eating the wings, stuffed potatoes and cheese sticks. I paused for a few minutes and observed what was happening around me. I was right, the platter was still half full, but no one was reaching for the crunchy creations. I had an overwhelming desire to reach for another, but offered the platter to those around me first. No one wanted any more. Most telling me they were full. So I put the question on the table "Please tell me how you know enough is enough? What does satisfaction feel like to you? How do you know you are full?" The group found the question amusing and everyone offered his or here interpretation. After a long discussion my son who had not said a word since arriving. He looked at me and said momma, you are asking the wrong question. You don't stop when you are full, you stop when you are no longer hungry." I sat there digesting what my little Einstein had said. For several years I have shared this story and many have said we have stumbled on the key. It is pretty easy to determine if your stomach is grumbling hunger pangs, if you feel shaky or have the beginning of a hunger headache. It is not so easy to feel or describe the satisfaction of being just right, Not stuffed. But just right. So I focus on not being hungry and now have a much bigger handle on when to stop eating. I think about it like a traffic light. Red light means stop, I am no longer hungry, yellow light is to be cautions the hunger is dissipating and it its time to begin to push away. Green light is hunger and time to eat.

The second reason to eat is the taste of the food. If you are eating for the taste of the food the last bite will not taste any different than the first bite, so limit your bites. If you are eating for the taste of the food, limit to three bites or tastes.

Our family has found a great tool for figuring out a lot of things: The 1-10 scale! Instead of saying "Do you want to do this, that or the other..." we'll ask

"On a scale of 1-10, what are your thoughts/feelings on this, that or the other?"

For so many things, a yes or no just doesn't work! This 1-10 scale has easily clarified a whole lot of miscommunication and disappointments because it's such a safe way of expressing yourself honestly and inoffensively.

A scale of 1-10 can measure lots of things, including danger zones for healthy eating. I've determined that a No. 10 zone (being most dangerous) is when I'm procrastinating, or bored. It's not that I'm hungry, I'd just rather prowl around the kitchen eating than get organized and down to business. (Cleaning up after a meal is another No. 10 for me.)

You probably have your own No. 10 zones. It's helpful to know them. Identifying safe zones matters too. To face my danger zones, I'm challenging myself to listen to my hunger, watch the clock and to schedule meals and snacks 3-4 hours apart so that when I do eat, there's a real reason.

How do you know when you're really hungry? Here's a 1-10 scale that has helped me and others. The time to eat is the mid-range, 4-6. The low 1-3 numbers are dangerous because we eat too much too fast. The upper 8-10 range is dangerous because we're eating on an emotional level.

The 1-10 Scale of Hunger:

1 - Starving, dizzy, head ache

2 - Ravenous

3 - Stomach pangs and growling

4 - Slightly hungry

5 - Neutral

6 - Satisfied

7 - Slightly full

8 - Feeling like I ate too much food

9 - Stuffed and uncomfortable

10 - Extreme nausea, painful

Well, I know the whole range intimately, you probably will too soon! No finger pointing! No guilt! Instead, we'll make eating at the 4-7 range scale second nature in our healthy eating lifestyle.

We can say good bye to those big numbers with the 1-10 scale. And soon we will say good bye to some pounds too. And remember, the point my youngest made about when to stop eating. It has little to do with being full or satisfied in his mind. It is all about when you are no longer hungry. What a difference this makes in my choices.

This week continue to journal what you are eating, tune into the signals you have for hunger and satisfaction. If you kept a journal and tracked your calories during the first week, concentrating on eating as you normally do; you have been able to determine approximately the calories it takes to maintain your current weight. Decrease you calories from the first week by 500 a day, for a 3500 a week deficit. If you are eating for taste three bites is the stopping point. We sometimes want the taste of a certain food. These are usually high calorie treats. There is a place for treats and weight loss, so recognize them for what they are and enjoy every bite. Have the goal of stopping at just 3 bites of those high calorie treats such as pie, cake, and fudge. We definitely do not want to start off with those types of foods when we are very hungry.

Week THREE

Move a little More.

If you are like most of us today, every minute is filled with a commitment. Whether the commitment is personal, family, work or social there doesn't seem to be time to join a gym or begin an exercise program. (Especially if it is not part of your adult life, currently.) The good news is that you do not have to join anything. Even a modest amount of added movement can yield results.

Having an exercise routine, even if it is just for a few minutes a day can curb appetites and stress related eating. JUST...Take a walk.

Tips to increase activity.

When going to pick up the paper before morning coffee, walk the length of your driveway twice, then walk down and pick up the paper.

When doing errands in the office, use the stairs instead of the elevator.

Commit to delivering one phone message in the office in person.

Store snack type food on another floor of your home, away from the kitchen and when having a snack take only one portion.

When shopping in the grocery store take one lap around the perimeter of the store before getting your shopping cart.

If you spend a lot of time in front of the TV, place hand weights or 2 bottles of water beside your chair. During commercials commit to lifting the weights, bottles over your head for the entire commercial.

While working on the computer, commit to standing and stretching for 2 minutes every hour.

Make adding exercise a group event; invite a neighbor, spouse, child, and coworker to form a walking group.

Commit to walking just 10 minutes a day. Once you have started moving aim to increase your activity to at least 30 minutes each day.

If you commit to increasing your movement on most days you can expend calories in a year that is between 4 and 10 pounds of weight loss.

If you add 2 hours of exercise a week, that is adding movement 17 minutes a day, in small burst you can lose up to 12 pounds a year. Small changes yield big results.

Ways to Burn 100 calories

1. Give your dog a bath for 25 minutes.

2. Tread water in the deep end of the pool for 25 minutes.

3. 780 jumping jacks will burn off 100 calories.

4. When filling up your gas tank in your car always use self-service; 6 times will burn off 100 calories.

5. Did you know that using a hula hoop for 20 minutes will burn 100 calories?

6. 20 minutes in a kayak will burn 100 calories.

7. All it takes is 15 minutes of leisurely laps to burn 100 calories.

8. Take your time preparing meals; chop veggies and slave over stove for 35 minutes.

9. Jump rope for 10 minutes.

10. You burn 100 calories every 20 minutes golfing.

Are you beginning to think of creative ways to sneak in some steps. I love couch aerobics. I commit to the time I spend in front of the television to not watch commercials. When a commercial is on, it is the perfect time to run upstairs to check on the laundry. Maybe look out the front door at the weather, or just flex some of my muscles. How are you finding ways to sneak in a little movement?

Week FOUR

Do you eat breakfast???

If you answer No, then please begin with something as early as possible in the day. To jump start your metabolism; you need to begin with a nutritious breakfast. You can not run a car without energy, (gas or petroleum) and neither will your body run without energy (food). For years, in an attempt to conserve as many calories in a day as possible, I would fast as long as possible. This not only slowed my metabolism, but it also made me feel listless and lethargic. Then when I could last no longer without food. I would eat what was fast, and not what was healthy.

If you answered Yes, then the tip for you is to make the breakfast work its best for you. Choose high fiber and protein. I recommend trying to consume 8 to 10 grams of fiber in this meal. This is very easy to do with the high fiber cereals available today. I also recommend that you replace fruit juice with the whole fruit. It is more filling and has more fiber. Breakfast is the most important meal of the day. Make smart choices. Avoid commercially prepared muffins, read labels and substituted fresh fruit and oatmeal.

Wake up a little earlier each morning to give yourself a little time for breakfast, if this is not possible create a morning break box, filled with high fiber breakfast bars, dried fruit, and oatmeal. Have something healthy with your morning coffee. Also, stock the refrigerator with low- fat yogurt smoothies for on the way into the office.

For an occasional treat try a whole grain waffle or pancake; and opt for sugar free syrup. The syrup will save up to 150 calories per serving.

Munching on the Road

Despite the proof, most of us devote almost no time to breakfast. Fact is, most of us eat it on the go. Researchers say that a large majority of Americans eat breakfast in their cars. This isn't ideal, but if you must eat on the go, try to get the most mileage out of your food. Here are five healthy mobile suggestions:

1. Fruit

The possibilities are endless. Try apples, bananas, pears, peaches, or nectarines. Fruit is low in calories and contains some of the fiber necessary for a healthy diet. Eating it early in the morning will give you a head start on your daily servings of fruit and vegetables.

2. High-fiber toast

Just pop bread in the toaster before you head into the shower, and grab it on your way out the door. Spread a little peanut butter on top for a good dose of protein. Or enjoy some sugar free jam. YUM!

3. Breakfast or cereal bar.

All you need to do is unwrap them. But read the label; some are about as nutritious as a candy bar. I have listed some favorites in a later chapter.

4. Hard-boiled egg

The perfect portable anytime food. Eggs are highly nutritious, full of protein and a good source of Vitamin B-12 and riboflavin. And they're easy to cook ahead of time, then just grab and go. They even have ready to eat boiled eggs in your grocery store fridge. They are even peeled for you.

5. Smoothie

For late-risers, here's a breakfast option you can toss into the blender the night before, refrigerate, and whip up just before you walk out the door: Before bed, combine 1/2 cup of nonfat yogurt, a banana, five strawberries and 1/2 cup fruit juice in a blender. In the morning, add ice and blend until smooth.

Dining at Your Desk

If you'd rather eat at your desk, here are three easy meals:

1. Oatmeal, cream of wheat or grits

It's simple to keep packets of these in your desk. Just add hot water and you're set. All three are high in carbohydrates and fiber and relatively low in calories. There is even some sugar free varieties available.

2. Breakfast sandwich.

This is worth it for the high nutritional payoff—and you can make ahead, keep in the fridge and reheat. Toast a light, high-fiber English muffin, top it with three scrambled egg whites, onions and a strip of bacon. You're getting fiber, protein and carbohydrates all in one. There is also some ready made varieties in the freezer section, watch the label but we are fortunate to have some great choices.

3. Low-fat yogurt.

The classic healthy stand-by you can just grab from the fridge. Yogurt is also a good source of calcium. Bulk it out with fresh fruit such as strawberries or melons.

Week FIVE

Variety is the spice of life

The majority of your calories should come from fruit and vegetables. Add these to main dishes; try a variety of colors. Chose beans and legumes as protein sources.

Keep fresh vegetables and fruits in the front of your refrigerator. Start your evening meal with a salad. Chose a light dressing (one with 45 calories or less per serving) or vinaigrette and use one serving of the dressing. A salad is only as healthy as its toppings. If you choose cheese. Opt for low or nonfat. I recommend avoiding the cheese and croutons all together. Chicken, egg and tuna salads are not the salads I recommend. Salads are the fresh green leafy vegetables with fruit and vegetable toppings. They are full of fiber and make you feel fuller, longer. Have your dressing on the side and dip your fork into the dressing and then pick up the salad.

The focus this week is on getting a minimum of five fruits and veggies daily.

Remember the previous weeks tips and keep them up, doesn't it feel empowering to take control of your choices.

Great salad starters!

Salad Greens (Romaine, Iceberg, Spring Mix, Etc.) - 3 cups = 25 calories, <0.5g fat, 3g fiber

Tomatoes - 1/2 cup = 15 calories, <0.5g fat, 1g fiber

Cucumbers - 1/2 cup = 8 calories, 0g fat, <0.5g fiber

Mushrooms - 1/2 cup = 8 calories, 0g fat, <0.5g fiber

Pepper Strips - 1/2 cup = 12 calories, 0g fat, 1g fiber

Pepperoncinis, Jalapenos, Sweet Peppers - 1/4 cup = 10 calories, <0.5g fat, 0.5g fiber

Alfalfa Sprouts - 1/2 cup = 5 calories, 0g fat, <0.5g fiber

Salsa - 1/4 cup = 25 calories, <0.5g fat, 1g fiber

Vinegar (Red Wine, Balsamic, Etc.) - 2 tbsp. = 15 calories, 0g fat, 0g fiber

Fat-Free, Reduced Calorie Dressings - 2 tbsp. = 40 calories, <0.5g fat, 0g fiber

Week SIX

Snacking

There is Nothing wrong with a snack, just make sure you are snacking related to hunger and not another reason.

Portion control here is the key. Buy single serving size snacks, or make your own. Choose a healthy snack. If it is salt you crave opt for 94% fat free or air popped popcorn, if you can't resist potato chips choose baked. The average 7-ounce bag of regular potato chips has around 1100 calories. The same size bag of baked chips has around 800. Let's assume you currently eat a bag of chips a week. By choosing the baked chips you are saving 15,600 calories a year. That is 4 and 1/2 pounds you lost in one year. And you still ate your chips.

Is Chocolate what you just can't resist? You can't have it every day and lose weight, but don't deprive yourself from the occasional treat. Chose a single serving and enjoy it. Read labels because all chocolate is not created equal. You can probably find a lower calorie choice that will suit your taste buds.

Another way to get the chocolate taste is sugar free hot cocoa or chocolate flavored sugar free coffees.

Try fresh fruit dipped in chocolate. You are having a fruit snack and a chocolate fix all at once.

Snacking can be a beneficial tool to promote weight loss, it can prevent overeating from allowing yourself to not get too hungry between meals. Also, snacking can help to keep your metabolism running. Pay close attention to when you snack and the choices you are making. Are you using snacks as meal replacements? Plan for your snacks. Make the most of your choices. Picking and munching on snacks that are not planned can quickly add up to a large number of calories.

One Dozen Grab 'n Go Snacks

1. Breakfast cereal, dry or with milk and fruit. Try low sugar, multigrain kinds. You want at least three grams of dietary fiber. Keep single serving boxes on hand.

2. No-sugar-added applesauce, sliced peaches in their own juice, and other single serving fruits.

3. Fresh fruit, such as pears, apples, oranges, nectarines, peaches, kiwi, grapes, and strawberries.

4. Mixed nuts and a single serving can of tomato juice.

5. Dried apricots, apples, nectarines, etcetera. Keep portions modest to control calories as dried fruits can be high in sugar.

6. Low-fat milk and a homemade or store-bought low-fat, whole grain muffin. Keep frozen and microwave muffin briefly before eating. Be careful with jumbo-sized muffins!

7. Popcorn (2-1/2 cups) with margarine (1-1/2 teaspoons) or butter-flavored spray.

8. Turkey ham (1 oz.) and 1 soft bread stick with spaghetti sauce (2 tbs.).

9. Saltine crackers (4) and part-skim Mozzarella cheese stick (1 oz.).

10. A turkey kabob: turkey & cheese cubes (.5 oz. each) with pretzel sticks and low-fat milk (8 oz.)

11. Packaged, ready-to-eat vegetables such as baby carrots, broccoli florets, and cauliflower pieces with a low-fat dip (2 tbs.)

12. Chopped vegetables from your own kitchen such as red and green bell peppers, jicama, carrot and celery sticks, snow peas, button mushrooms, and/or broccoli with non-fat ranch dressing.

Week SEVEN

Healthy Grains

Choose foods made from Whole grains, this should be listed as the first ingredient on the label. Opt for brown rice or barley. Avoid refined grains, such as white bread. Eating whole grains help to make you feel fuller, longer. Keep instant oatmeal on hand for breakfast or a snack. Select the darkest bread, when you have a choice. Enjoy air-popped or fat free microwave popcorn as a snack. Yes, popcorn is considered a grain.

Foods that are high in fiber - whole grains, fruits, nuts, and vegetables - help you feel full while providing essential nutrients your body needs to metabolize calories. Both factors have been shown to be beneficial for healthy weight management. There are two types of fiber, and your body needs both. Insoluble fiber acts like a broom and soluble fiber acts like a sponge.

Increase whole grains in your diet by choosing high-fiber cereals, eating oatmeal for breakfast, and opting for whole-grain breads and pastas. Research suggests that whole grains such as oats may help control appetite because soluble fiber absorbs water, significantly slowing the digestive process. As a result, you feel fuller longer. Studies show that people are more successful at losing weight and keeping it off when they eat breakfast regularly. Fresh fruits and vegetables are an excellent source of fiber, and some choices are high in both soluble and insoluble types of fiber. Pears are a good example.

Fiber Content in Common Foods

Here is a list of common foods, according to serving size and their fiber content. You may notice slight differences in fiber content on food packages, in reference books or in brochures about food and health. That may be due to how the fiber was determined (there are a few methods), or that serving size varied, etc. Some sources give the precise fiber content to the decimal (3.2 grams, for instance), while others round up (or down) to the nearest whole number. The numbers in the chart below are rounded, unless they contain less than 1 gram per serving. Other foods such as packages breads have labels, be careful to look at the portion and determine the amount of calories and fiber in the amount of the food you choose to eat.

FOOD		FIBER
Apple (with peel)	1 medium	3
Banana	1 medium	3
Blueberries	1 cup	4
Cantaloupe	1 cup	1
Orange	1 medium	3
Grapefruit	1 medium	3
Pear (with peel)	1 medium	4
Pineapple	1 cup	2
Raspberries	1 cup	8
Prunes (dried)	½ cup	6

Asparagus	(5 medium, cooked)	2
Kidney beans (cooked)	½ cup	6
Pinto beans	½ cup	8
Broccoli (cooked)	½ cup	2
Carrots	½ cup	2
Cauliflower (cooked)	½ cup	2
Sweet potato, w. skin (baked)	1 medium	5
White potato, w. skin (baked)	1 medium	3
Spinach, frozen, cooked, drained	½ cup	3
Tomato	1 medium	1
Peanuts, dry-roasted	½ cup	6

Week EIGHT

Survival of the WEEKEND

Do you feel like you are motivated to make healthy choices until the weekend rolls around? Then you forget the tips and blow the week's hard work? Healthy choices are possible on the weekend with just a little tweaking of the choices you are already making. This is some helpful ideas.

Opt for home made low fat cheese pizza or frozen low fat instead of the traditional take out and you will save 300-400 calories per slice.

You can burn calories having fun. Take up a new activity.

Overate?? Just get over it. You have a plan to make small changes and they are working... just get back to the plan.

The weekend does not have to revolve around food, enjoy the people in your life. Put yourself in situations to meet new people.

Limit alcohol, bars are not known for the healthy foods they serve. Choose your alcohol carefully, there is a huge calorie variant between a glass of red wine and a piña colada. Do your calorie homework when it comes to alcohol.

Dining in restaurants can spell disaster to healthful eating. Before heading out the door, check for a web site for a restaurant guide. Call ahead and ask that the menu be faxed to check choices.

Seafood is usually the better choice. Avoid fried, blackened, sautéed, cream, and butter sauces. Better choices include boiled, broiled, and steamed.

Most meals away from home include enough calories for 2 meals. Consider sharing an entree, or take half home for the next day.

Control your impulses at a buffet by first walking completely around the tables and see the choices. Chose a salad first and then go for the other choices. Do not deprive yourself of a food you really enjoy. INSTEAD control the portion. At home you would never have 3 plates of food. Why consider this at a buffet? Beware of shinny vegetables, many times they are covered in butter and that is a quick way to add up calories, and think you are making a much lighter choice.

Other tips include asking for a to go box at the beginning of your meal, instead of at the end. You can safely place a portion out of sight for another reasonable meal the next day. I frequently divide an entrée with my spouse or dining partner. You can also order an appetizer for your meal. Always remember the lightening up tips and leave the high fat condiments like mayonnaise and cheese off. This can save hundreds of calories.

Week NINE

Tools of the trade

Let me recommend first that you get to know your kitchen. There are a few items that will make food preparation easier and save calories.

If you do not own a crock-pot slow cooker, it is time to purchase one.

Make every recipe in non-stick pans.

Purchase a food scale and limit portions to one.

Plastic containers for fresh fruits and vegetables are a necessity. Prepare the foods as soon as you come in from the grocery store. They will be ready for snacking and no excuse of it takes too long to prepare.

Get to know the spice isle. Use these to add flavor. Experiment and find what you enjoy. REMEMBER Spices add no calories to foods.

To help you get healthy meals on the table in minutes, lets adopt the idea of *Cook Once, Eat All Week*. Just think of all the free time you'll have! (With the current cost of electricity and gas, even putting a few extra pieces of chicken on the grill can save some big bucks in the energy department!

Eight Excellent Reasons to Cook Ahead

1. You lead a busy life. Cooking ahead gives you more time in the evenings to do whatever else you do.

2. Have a marathon cooking session on Sunday and you won't have to cook again all week long.

3. You can make it a fun, weekend family affair. Assign children age-appropriate tasks like slicing and dicing or sautéing and grilling.

4. If it's 7 p.m., you're hungry, and you still have to make dinner, you may be more prone to nibbling while your meal cooks—a practice that can be counterproductive to weight loss.

5. Having a well-stocked refrigerator and freezer minimizes last-minute takeout temptations.

6. Ready-made meals stored in individual- or family-sized containers make for simple portion control (not to mention easy cleanup).

7. Shopping, prepping and cooking for several similar recipes at once (cutting veggies for a soup and a salad, or grilling chicken that can be used for a pasta dish and wrap sandwiches, for example) saves time.

8. There's a financial advantage: Buying groceries in larger quantities and making only one trip to the supermarket each week saves money in the long run.

To lighten up recipes, try some of these substitutions.

The key is to cut 500 calories a day, If you can lighten the recipe and still have the flavor it seems to me the best place to save those calories.

INSTEAD OF USING:	TRY THIS:
Bacon	Canadian bacon, turkey based sausage
Beef broth	Vegetable stocks
Beef Frank	Chicken or Turkey frank
Bologna/ Frankfurter/ Sausage	Chicken/Turkey/Lean, thinly-sliced beef
Butter on toast	Apple butter, preserves
Butter on vegetables	Molly McButter, Yogurt sauces, spices/herbs
Cakes w/frosting	Angel food cake w/fresh fruit
Canned fruits	Canned in own juice, fresh fruits
Catsup	Tomato sauce
Cheesecake	Cheesecake made w/low fat cream cheese
Chicken breast/skin	Chicken w/o breast/skin
Corn chips	Make your own tortilla chips
Cream based soups	Tomato based soups

Cream Cheese	Nonfat cream cheese product, drained low/nonfat yogurt
Cream	Skim milk or evaporated skim milk
Creamed cottage cheese	Low fat cottage cheese
Creamed vegetables	Seasoned vegetables
Eggs	Egg substitute, more whites, less yolks
French Toast	Pancake
Fried foods	Baked or broiled foods
Frozen custard	Frozen yogurt
Fudge Toping	Chocolate syrup, Vashon products
Glazed donut	Cake donut
Ground beef	Extra-lean ground beef
Hot fudge sundae	Frozen lowfat yogurt with fruit
Ice Cream	Ice Milk, nonfat frozen yogurt
Jams & Syrups	Unsweetened berries
Nuts as snacks	Pretzels, plain popcorn w/lowfat seasoning
Oil for sautéing	Water
Oil in quick breads	Fruit juice or nectar or sparkling water
Oreos/Chocolate chip cookies	Animal crackers, vanilla wafers, graham crackers

Pan Drippings	Bouillon
Peanuts	Water chestnuts
Pecan pie	Custard pie
Pie crusts	Crushed bran Chex, shredded wheat or whole wheat crackers
Pie crusts for quiches	Cooked brown rice brushed with egg white
Popcorn in oil	Lowfat popcorn, air popped popcorn
Potato chips/ Popcorn	Reduced fat substitutes, pretzels
Ramen Oriental Noodles (pork)	Chicken Noodles Soup
Refined flour	Whole wheat flour
Regular salad dressing	Reduced calorie/nonfat dressings, lemon juice, vinegar
Ritz crackers, Waverly crackers	Whole grain crackers
Salt	Herbs and spices
Snickers Bar	Three Musketeers Bar
Sour Cream	Nonfat and lowfat yogurt, nonfat and lowfat cottage cheese, nonfat sour cream products, mock sour cream
Sugar or honey	Apple or pineapple juice, boiled down to syrup consistency

Sugared cereals	Puffed wheat, rice, Cheerios & higher fiber cereals
Tang	Fresh orange or orange juice
Typical ice cream bar	Frozen fruit juice bar

Week TEN

Get your Dairy products

If digesting dairy is a problem, consider lactose free products. Include 2-3 servings of dairy products daily. The protein will help you to feel satisfied longer.

Let's talk ice cream... the average cup has 300-500 calories. There are so many frozen treats with a percentage of those calories on the market today. Several are listed in favorite snack foods. Try one and the calorie savings are tremendous. If on the occasion you can't live without a true ice cream cone. Do it, but control it. Visit your favorite ice cream parlor and have a single scoop. Never bring home a half-gallon, the temptation to over indulge is often too much for most of us.

If you switch from full fat milk to 2% you will save 20 calories a serving, go to fat free and save an additional 30 calories. A Low fat cheese switch saves 30-50 calories per serving. Switching to low fat yogurt saves 50-75 calories. If you switch 3 dairy servings of the full fat kind with a fat free or low fat choice you will save 150- 200 calories a day. That is about 1/2 pound per week.

Is this switch worth it for you? It was for me, and after a short time I began to prefer the fat free taste. Try it for a week and decide for yourself.

Week ELEVEN

Dining Out

Dining Out can present a challenge for all of us. Partially due to gigantic portions and limitless varieties of tempting, unhealthy foods. But in today's society, we dine out more than ever before, and you shouldn't have to give that up now that you're trying to lose weight. By learning how to incorporate healthy restaurant eating into your plan, you'll be setting yourself up for a lifetime of success.

Prepare yourself before you leave your home.

Arm yourself with knowledge about the menu by researching the calories online.

Don't arrive starving.

While it's probably a good idea to eat lower calorie meals that day to budget some extra calories for your dinner, don't show up famished.

Tips for dining out

I always ask to place my order first, as to not be swayed by what others are choosing.

Drink plenty of water before and during the meal.

Ask for foods to be prepared withOUT oils, sauces or butter.

Order double veggies instead of high calorie dishes.

Limit alcoholic beverages.

Relax. Don't approach the dinner with trepidation. You're not denying yourself anything, you're making choices about your life. And you're sharing a meal with those you love, whether that is your honey, your family, or a group of friends. How could it get any better than that?

Ask for what you want. **Scan the menu to create your own dinner.**

If you want the fish, but don't want the cream sauce, ask for it to be served with the salsa that comes with the chicken, or the fresh herbs from the pasta. If you want veal but don't want it drenched in butter, ask for it with lemon juice and herbs.

Fancier restaurants prepare dishes to order, so it's no problem. Less fancy dining establishments are often willing to make changes too. There's no harm in asking!

The same goes for the sides.

That shrimp dish you want might come with potato skins, but the roast chicken comes with grilled asparagus. Just ask for the shrimp with asparagus.

Tell the chef not to "finish" the sauce.

Chefs sometimes swirl butter into a sauce before it's served. Ask if the sauce can be plain, fresh and bright, not "finished."

Ask for recommendations.

If the chef cannot accommodate you, ask your waiter to suggest an alternative, lighter preparation. But ask for what you want the way you want it.

Order simpler food prepared light.

In terms of calories, grilled is usually better than fried; baked is better than braised.

Ask for your meal to be divided, or a to-go box at the beginning of the meal.

Meals these days are often served in enormous portions. Ask the waiter to divide yours *before* it's served and put one half in a take-home bag that's reserved for you in the kitchen. That way you'll have dinner the next day too.

Cut things out during the meal. Forego the cocktail, which can be loaded with sugar, and have a glass of red wine instead.

Ask for lemon juice or vinegar on the salad.

Ask for cocktail sauce or chutney on your baked potato, rather than butter and sour cream.

Share. You can split an appetizer, a salad or a dessert. It's very romantic to share a dish with someone you love! Many times if it is not a loved one, they also want to cut some calories. So offer to SHARE.

The following tool is to introduce you to the information available from Restaurant menu's. Sometimes we think we are making healthy choices when in actuality we could make a much better one, if we look at the nutritional information. Most restaurants provide this tool for you. Ask for it from your favorite dining spot and get to know the best choice for you. It is also available on line from most restaurants. Do some homework before you head out the door.

Approximate calories in some favorite restaurants, as listed on their menu nutritional information.

Boston Market

Entrees
1/4 White meat chicken w/no skin or wing (170 cal/4 g fat)
1/4 White meat chicken w/skin & wing (280 cal/12 g fat)
1/4 Dark meat chicken w/no skin (190 cal/10 g fat)
1/4 Dark meat chicken w/skin (320 cal/21 g fat)
1/2 Chicken w/skin (590 cal/33 g fat)
Skinless Rotisserie Turkey Breast (170 cal/1 g fat)
Boston Hearth Ham (210 cal/9 g fat)
Meat Loaf & Chunky Tomato Sauce (370 cal/18 g fat)
Meat Loaf & Brown Gravy (390 cal/22 g fat)
Chicken Pot Pie (780 cal/46 g fat/61)
Chunky Chicken Salad (370 cal/27 g fat)
Teriyaki Chicken 1/4 dark w/skin (380 cal/21 g fat)
Teriyaki Chicken 1/4 white w/skin (340 cal/12 g fat)
Tabasco BBQ drumstick (130 cal/6 g fat)
Tabasco BBQ wings (110 cal/7 g fat)
Triple Topped Chicken (470 cal/22 g fat)
Southwest Savory Chicken (400 cal/15 g fat)

Soups & Salads
Southwest Chicken Salad (920 cal/68 g fat/8 g fiber)
Caesar Salad Entree (510 cal/42 g fat/3 g fiber)
Caesar Side Salad (200 cal/17 g fat/1 g fiber)
Caesar Salad w/o dressing (230 cal/12 g fat/3 g fiber)
Chicken Caesar Salad (650 cal/45 g fat/3 g fiber)
Tossed Salad w/Fat Free Ranch (160 cal/2.5 g fat)
Tossed Salad w/Old Venice Dressing (340 cal/27 g fat)
Tossed Salad w/Caesar Dressing (380 cal/31 g fat)
Chicken Noodle Soup (130 cal/4.5 g fat/1 g fiber)
Chicken Tortilla Soup (220 cal/11 g fat/2 g fiber)
Potato Soup (270 cal/16 g fat)
Tomato Bisque (280 cal/23 g fat)
Chicken Chili (220 cal/7 g fat)

Sandwiches
Chicken SW w/cheese & sauce (750 cal/33 g fat/5 g fiber)
Chicken SW w/no cheese & sauce (430 cal/4.5 g fat/5 g

fiber)
Chicken Salad Sandwich **(680 cal/30 g fat/4 g fiber)**
Turkey SW w/cheese & sauce **(710 cal/28 g fat/4 g fiber)**
Turkey SW w/no cheese & sauce **(400 cal/3.5 g fat/4 g fiber)**
Ham SW w/cheese & sauce **(750 cal/34 g fat/5 g fiber)**
Ham SW w/no cheese & sauce **(440 cal/8 g fat/4 g fiber)**
Meat Loaf Sandwich w/cheese **(860 cal/33 g fat/6 g fiber)**
Meat Loaf Sandwich w/no cheese **(690 cal/21 g fat/6 g fiber)**
Turkey Club Sandwich **(650 cal/26 g fat)**
Open Faced Turkey Sandwich **(500 cal/12 g fat)**
Open Faced Meat Loaf Sandwich **(760 cal/35 g fat)**
BBQ Chicken Sandwich **(540 cal/9 g fat)**
Pastry SW - Broccoli, Chicken, Cheddar **(690 cal/47 g fat)**
Pastry SW - Ham & Cheddar **(640 cal/41 g fat)**
Pastry SW - Italian Chicken **(630 cal/41 g fat)**
Pastry Sandwich - BBQ Chicken **(640 cal/39 g fat)**
Hot and Cold Side Dishes (3/4 cup unless noted)
Baked Sweet Potato **(460 cal/7 g fat)**
BBQ Baked Beans **(270 cal/5 g fat/9 g fiber)**
Black Beans & Rice, 1 cup **(300 cal/10 g fat)**
Broccoli Cauliflower Au Gratin **(200 cal/11 g fat)**
Broccoli w/Red Peppers **(60 cal/3.5 g fat)**
Broccoli Rice Casserole **(240 cal/12 g fat)**
Butternut Squash **(160 cal/6 g fat/3 g fiber)**
Chicken Gravy, 2 tbsp **(15 cal/1 g fat/0 g fiber)**
Creamed Spinach **(260 cal/20 g fat/2 g fiber)**
Green Beans **(80 cal/6 g fat)**
Green Beans Casserole **(130 cal/9 g fat/2 g fiber)**
Mashed Potatoes, 2/3 cup, w/gravy **(190 cal/9 g fat/2 g fiber)**
Honey Glazed Carrots **(280 cal/15 g fat)**
Hot Cinnamon Apples **(250 cal/4.5 g fat/3 g fiber)**
Macaroni & Cheese **(280 cal/11 g fat/1 g fiber)**
New Potatoes, lowfat **(130 cal/2.5 g fat/2 g fiber)**
Oven Roasted Potato Planks, 5 **(180 cal/5 g fat)**

Red Beans & Rice, 1 cup (260 cal/5 g fat)
Rice Pilaf, 2/3 cup (180 cal/5 g fat/2 g fiber)
Savory Stuffing (310 cal/12 g fat/3 g fiber)
Squash Casserole (330 cal/24 g fat)
Steamed Vegetables, 2/3 cup (35 cal/.5 g fat/3 g fiber)
Sweet Potato Casserole (280 cal/18 g fat)
Whole Kernel Corn (180 cal/4 g fat/2 g fiber)
Zucchini Marinara (60 cal/3 g fat/2 g fiber)
Cranberry Relish (370 cal/5 g fat/5 g fiber)
Cole Slaw (300 cal/19 g fat/3 g fiber)
Chunky Cinnamon Applesauce (250 cal/0 g fat)
Coyote Bean Salad (190 cal/9 g fat)
Fruit Salad (70 cal/.5 g fat/2 g fiber)
Old Fashioned Potato Salad (340 cal/24 g fat)

Baked Goods

Brownie, 1 piece (450 cal/27 g fat/3 g fiber)
Chocolate Chip Cookie (340 cal/17 g fat/1 g fiber)
Oatmeal Raisin Cookie (320 cal/13 g fat/1 g fiber)
Honey Wheat Roll (150 cal/2 g fat/2 g fiber)
Cinnamon Apple Pie, 1/5 of pie (390 cal/23 g fat)
Corn Bread, 1 loaf (200 cal/6 g fat/1 g fiber)

Burger King

WHOPPER Sandwiches
WHOPPER Sandwich **(670 cal/39 g fat/3 g fiber)**
WHOPPER Sandwich (w/o Mayo) **(510 cal/22 g fat/3 g fiber)**
WHOPPER Sandwich with Cheese **(760 cal/47 g fat/3 g fiber)**
WHOPPER Sandwich, Cheese w/o Mayo **(600 cal/30 g fat/3 g fiber)**
DOUBLE WHOPPER Sandwich **(900 cal/57 g fat/3 g fiber)**
DOUBLE WHOPPER Sandwich w/o Mayo **(740 cal/39g fat/3g fiber)**
DOUBLE WHOPPER Sandwich Cheese **(990 cal/64 g fat/3g fiber)**
DOUBLE WHOPPER Sandwich w Cheese (w/o Mayo) **(830 cal/47 g fat/3 g fiber)**
TRIPLE WHOPPER Sandwich **(1130 cal/74 g fat/3 g fiber)**
TRIPLE WHOPPER Sandwich (w/o Mayo) **(980 cal/57 g fat/3gfiber)**
TRIPLE WHOPPER Sandwich with Cheese **(1230 cal/82 g fat/3 g fiber)**
TRIPLE WHOPPER Sandwich with Cheese (w/o Mayo) **(1070 cal/65 g fat/3 g fiber)**
WHOPPER JR. Sandwich **(370 cal/21 g fat/2 g fiber)**
WHOPPER JR. Sandwich (w/o Mayo) **(290 cal/12 g fat/2 g fiber)**
WHOPPER JR. Sandwich with Cheese **(410 cal/24 g fat/2 g fiber)**
WHOPPER JR. Sandwich with Cheese (w/o Mayo) **(330cal/16g fat/2g fiber)**
Bacon (1 strip) **(15 cal/1 g fat/0 g fiber)**
Fire-Grilled Burgers
Hamburger **(290 cal/12 g fat/1 g fiber)**
Cheeseburger **(330 cal/16 g fat/1 g fiber)**
Double Hamburger **(410 cal/21 g fat/1 g fiber)**
Double Cheeseburger **(500 cal/29 g fat/1 g fiber)**
Bacon Cheeseburger **(360 cal/18 g fat/1 g fiber)**

Bacon Double Cheeseburger **(530 cal/31 g fat/1 g fiber)**
BK Double Stacker **(610 cal/39 g fat/1 g fiber)**
BK Triple Stacker **(800 cal/54 g fat/1 g fiber)**
BK Quad Stacker **(1000 cal/68 g fat/1 g fiber)**
The Angus Steak Burger **(640 cal/33 g fat/3 g fiber)**

Chicken, Fish & Veggie

TENDERGRILL Chicken Sandwich **(450 cal/10 g fat/4 g fiber)**
TENDERGRILL Chicken Sandwich (with Mayo) **(510 cal/19 g fat/4 g fiber)**
TENDERGRILL Chicken Sandwich (w/o Sauce) **(400 cal/7 g fat/4 g fiber)**
TENDERCRISP Chicken Sandwich **(780 cal/43 g fat/4 g fiber)**
Spicy TENDERCRISP Chicken Sandwich **(720 cal/36 g fat/5 g fiber)**
Spicy TENDERCRISP Chicken Sandwich (w/o Sauce) **(570 cal/21 g fat/4 g fiber)**
Original Chicken Sandwich **(660 cal/40 g fat/4 g fiber)**
Original Chicken Sandwich (w/o Mayo) **(450 cal/17 g fat/4 g fiber)**
CHICKEN TENDERS Kid's Meal (4 pc) **(170 cal/10 g fat/0 g fiber)**
CHICKEN TENDERS (5 pc) **(210 cal/12 g fat/0 g fiber)**
CHICKEN TENDERS Big Kid's Meal (6 pc) **(250 cal/15 g fat/0 g fiber)**
CHICKEN TENDERS (8 pc) **(340 cal/20 g fat/0 g fiber)**
Barbecue Dipping Sauce (1 oz) **(40 cal/0 g fat/0 g fiber)**
Honey Flavored Dipping Sauce (1 oz) **(90 cal/0 g fat/0 g fiber)**
Honey Mustard Dipping Sauce (1 oz) **(90 cal/6 g fat/0 g fiber)**
Sweet and Sour Dipping Sauce (1 oz) **(45 cal/0 g fat/0 g fiber)**
Ranch Dipping Sauce (1 oz) **(140 cal/15 g fat/0 g fiber)**
BK CHICKEN FRIES (6 pc) **(260 cal/15 g fat/2 g fiber)**
BK CHICKEN FRIES (9 pc) **(390 cal/23 g fat/3 g fiber)**

BK CHICKEN FRIES (12 pc) **(520 cal/31 g fat/4 g fiber)**
Buffalo Dipping Sauce (1 oz) **(80 cal/8 g fat/0 g fiber)**
BK BIG FISH Sandwich **(630 cal/30 g fat/4 g fibers)**
BK BIG FISH Sandwich (w/o Tartar Sauce) **(470 cal/13 g fat/3 g fiber)**
Spicy BK BIG FISH Sandwich **(620 cal/29 g fat/4 g fiber)**
BK VEGGIE Burger **(420 cal/16 g fat/7 g fiber)**
BK VEGGIE Burger (w/Cheese) **(470 cal/20 g fat/7 g fiber)**
BK VEGGIE Burger (w/o Mayo) **(340 cal/8 g fat/7 g fiber)**
Side Orders
MOTTS Strawberry Flavored Apple Sauce **(90 cal/0 g fat/0 g fiber)**
Onion Rings (small) **(150 cal/7 g fat/1 g fiber)**
Onion Rings (medium) **(320 cal/16 g fat/3 g fiber)**
Onion Rings (large) **(450 cal/22 g fat/4 g fiber)**
Onion Rings (king) **(520 cal/26 g fat/5 g fiber)**
Zesty Onion Ring Dipping Sauce (1 oz) **(150 cal/15 g fat/0 g fiber)**
CHEESY TOTS (small, 6 pc) **(210 cal/12 g fat/2 g fiber)**
CHEESY TOTS (medium, 9 pc) **(320 cal/18 g fat/2 g fiber)**
CHEESY TOTS (large, 12 pc) **(430 cal/24 g fat/3 g fiber)**
French Fries (small, salted) **(230 cal/13 g fat/2 g fiber)**
French Fries (medium, salted) **(360 cal/20 g fat/4 g fiber)**
French Fries (large, salted) **(500 cal/28 g fat/5 g fiber)**
French Fries (king, salted) **(600 cal/33 g fat/6 g fiber)**
French Fries (small, no salt added) **(230 cal/13 g fat/2 g fiber)**
French Fries (medium, no salt added) **(360 cal/20 g fat/4 g fiber)**
French Fries (large, no salt added) **(500 cal/28 g fat/5 g fiber)**
French Fries (king, no salt added) **(600 cal/33 g fat/6 g fiber)**
Ketchup (packet) **(10 cal/0 g fat/0 g fiber)**
Salads w/out dressing or garlic parmesan croutons)
Side Garden Salad **(15 cal/0 g fat/1 g fiber)**
TENDERGRILL Chicken Garden Salad **(240 cal/9 g fat/4 g

fiber)
TENDERCRISP Chicken Garden Salad **(400 cal/21 g fat/5 g fiber)**
Garden Salad (no chicken) **(90 cal/4 g fat/3 g fiber)**

Salad Dressings & Toppings

KEN'S Light Italian Dressing (2 oz) **(120 cal/11 g fat/0 g fiber)**
KEN'S Ranch Dressing (2 oz) **(190 cal/20 g fat/0 g fiber)**
KEN'S Creamy Caesar Dressing (2 oz) **(210 cal/21 g fat/0 g fiber)**
KEN'S Honey Mustard Dressing (2 oz) **(270 cal/23 g fat/0 g fiber)**
KEN'S Fat Free Ranch Dressing (2 oz) **(60 cal/0 g fat/2 g fiber)**
Garlic Parmesan Croutons **(60 cal/2 g fat/0 g fiber)**

Desserts

Dutch Apple Pie **(300 cal/13 g fat/1 g fiber)**
HERSHEY'S Sundae Pie **(310 cal/19 g fat/1 g fiber)**

Breakfast

CROISSAN'WICH Egg & Cheese **(300 cal/17 g fat/0 g fiber)**
CROISSAN'WICH Sausage & Cheese **(370 cal/25 g fat/0 g fiber)**
CROISSAN'WICH Sausage, Egg & Cheese **(410 cal/32 g fat/0 g fiber)**
CROISSAN'WICH Ham, Egg & Cheese **(340 cal/18 g fat/1 g fiber)**
CROISSAN'WICH Bacon, Egg & Cheese **(340 cal/20 g fat/0 g fiber)**
DOUBLE CROISSAN'WICH w/Sausage, Egg & Cheese **(680 cal/51 g fat/0 g fiber)**
DOUBLE CROISSAN'WICH w/Bacon, Egg & Cheese **(430 cal/27 g fat/0 g fiber)**
DOUBLE CROISSAN'WICH w/Ham, Egg & Cheese **(420 cal/23 g fat/1 g fiber)**
DOUBLE CROISSAN'WICH w/Sausage, Bacon, Egg & Cheese **(560 cal/39 g fat/0 g fiber)**
DOUBLE CROISSAN'WICH w/Ham, Bacon, Egg & Cheese **(420

cal/24 g fat/1 g fiber)
DOUBLE CROISSAN'WICH w/Ham, Sausage, Egg & Cheese **(550 cal/37 g fat/1 g fiber)**
Enormous Omelet Sandwich **(730 cal/45 g fat/2 g fiber)**
Ham Omelet Sandwich **(330 cal/14 g fat/1 g fiber)**
Sausage Biscuit **(390 cal/26 g fat/1 g fiber)**
Ham, Egg & Cheese Biscuit **(390 cal/22 g fat/1 g fiber)**
Sausage, Egg & Cheese Biscuit **(530 cal/37 g fat/1 g fiber)**
Bacon, Egg & Cheese Biscuit **(410 cal/25 g fat/1 g fiber)**
Hash Browns (small) **(260 cal/17 g fat/2 g fiber)**
Hash Browns (medium) **(430 cal/28 g fat/4 g fiber)**
Hash Browns (large) **(620 cal/40 g fat/6 g fiber)**
Cini-Minis **(390 cal/18 g fat/2 g fiber)**
Vanilla Icing (for Cini-minis) **(110 cal/3 g fat/0 g fiber)**
French Toast Sticks (3 piece) **(230 cal/12 g fat/1 g fiber)**
French Toast Sticks (5 piece) **(380 cal/19 g fat/2 g fiber)**
Fench Toast Kid's Meal (w/syrup) **(660 cal/22 g fat/3 g fiber)**
Grape Jam **(30 cal/0 g fat/0 g fiber)**
Strawberry Jam **(30 cal/0 g fat/0 g fiber)**
Breakfast Syrup **(80 cal/0 g fat/0 g fiber)**
Shakes
Vanilla Milk Shake (Kid's) **(310 cal/11 g fat/0 g fiber)**
Vanilla Milk Shake (small) **(400 cal/15 g fat/0 g fiber)**
Vanilla Milk Shake (medium) **(560 cal/21 g fat/0 g fiber)**
Vanilla Milk Shake (large) **(820 cal/30 g fat/0 g fiber)**
Vanilla Milk Shake (king) **(1070 cal/39 g fat/0 g fiber)**
Chocolate Milk Shake (kid's) **(370 cal/11 g fat/1 g fiber)**
Chocolate Milk Shake (small) **(470 cal/14 g fat/1 g fiber)**
Chocolate Milk Shake (medium) **(690 cal/20 g fat/2 g fiber)**
Chocolate Milk Shake (large) **(950 cal/29 g fat/2 g fiber)**
Chocolate Milk Shake (king) **(1260 cal/38 g fat/3 g fiber)**
Strawberry Milk Shake (kid's) **(360 cal/10 g fat/0 g fiber)**
Strawberry Milk Shake (small) **(460 cal/14 g fat/0 g fiber)**
Strawberry Milk Shake (medium) **(660 cal/19 g fat/0 g fiber)**
Strawberry Milk Shake (large) **(930 cal/28 g fat/0 g fiber)**

Strawberry Milk Shake (king) **(1230 cal/36 g fat/0 g fiber)**
Beverages
Coca Cola Classic (kids) **(110 cal/ g fat 0)**
Coca Cola Classic (small) **(140 cal/ g fat 0)**
Coca Cola Classic (medium) **(200 cal/ g fat 0)**
Coca Cola Classic (large) **(290 cal/ g fat 0)**
Coca Cola Classic (king) **(390 cal/ g fat 0)**
Sprite (kids) **(110 cal/ g fat 0)**
Sprite (small) **(140 cal/ g fat 0)**
Sprite (medium) **(200 cal/ g fat 0)**
Sprite (large) **(290 cal/ g fat 0)**
Sprite (king) **(390 cal/ g fat 0)**
Dr. Pepper (kids) **(110 cal/ g fat 0)**
Dr. Pepper (small) **(140 cal/ g fat 0)**
Dr. Pepper (medium) **(190 cal/ g fat 0)**
Dr. Pepper (large) **(280 cal/ g fat 0)**
Dr. Pepper (king) **(380 cal/ g fat 0)**
Diet Coke (kids) **(0 cal/ g fat/ 0)**
Diet Coke (small) **(0 cal/ g fat 0)**
Diet Coke (medium) **(0 cal/ g fat 0)**
Diet Coke (large) **(0 cal/ g fat/0 g)**
Diet Coke (king) **(5 cal/ g fat/0 g)**
BK JOE Regular Coffee (small) **(5 cal/0 g fat)**
BK JOE Regular Coffee (medium) **(10 cal/ g fat)**
BK JOE Regular Coffee (large) **(10 cal/ 0g fat)**
BK JOE Turbo Coffee (small) **(10 cal/ g fat 0)**
BK JOE Turbo Coffee (medium) **(10 cal/ g fat 0)**
BK JOE Turbo Coffee (large) **(15 cal/ g fat)**
BK JOE Decaf Coffee (small) **(5 cal/ g fat/0)**
BK JOE Decaf Coffee (medium) **(5 cal/ g fat/0)**
BK JOE Decaf Coffee (large) **(5 cal/ g fat/0)**
MINUTE MAID Apple Juice (6.67 oz) **(90 cal/ g fat 0)**
MINUTE MAID Orange Juice (8 oz) **(140 cal/ g fat 0)**
AQUAFINA Water (16 fl oz) **(0 cal/ g fat/0)**
ICEE COCA COLA (small) **(110 cal/ g fat 0)**
ICEE COCA COLA (medium) **(140 cal/ g fat 0)**
ICEE MINUTE MAID Cherry (small) **(110 cal/ g fat 0)**

ICEE MINUTE MAID Cherry (medium) **(140 cal/ g fat 0)**
Regional Menu Items (available in limited markets & participating restaurants)
Bagel **(230 cal/1 g fat/2 g fiber)**
Bagel w/Egg, Cheese, Ham (2 sl) **(400 cal/12 g fat/2 g fiber)**
Bagel w/Egg, Cheese, Sausage **(540 cal/27 g fat/2 g fiber)**
Bagel w/Egg, Cheese, Bacon (3 pc) **(130 cal/15 g fat/2 g fiber)**
Biscuit w/Chicken Fritter (Chicken Biscuit) **(370 cal/19 g fat/2 g fiber)**
Biscuit w/Steak (Chicken-Fried) **(400 cal/24 g fat/1 g fiber)**
Biscuit w/Gravy **(420 cal/23 g fat/1 g fiber)**
Biscuit w/Country Ham (1 sl) & Egg **(360 cal/19 g fat/1 g fiber)**
Biscuit w/Sausage, Bacon (3 pc), Egg & Cheese **(570 cal/40 g fat/1 g fiber)**
Biscuit w/Sausage, Ham (2 sl), Egg & Cheese **(550 cal/37 g fat/1 g fiber)**
Biscuit w/Double Ham (4 sl), Egg & Cheese **(400 cal/22 g fat/1 g fiber)**
Breakfast Burrito - Sausage, Egg, Cheese & Salsa **(330 cal/19 g fat/1 g fiber)**
Breakfast Burrito - Potato, Egg, Cheese & Salsa **(320 cal/17 g fat/1 g fiber)**
Breakfast Burrito - Bacon, Egg, Cheese & Salsa **(290 cal/16 g fat/1 g fiber)**
French Toast Sandwich (French Toast Rounds, Egg Omelet, Sausage, Cheese) **(620 cal/37 g fat/2 g fiber)**
French Toast Sandwich w/Bacon (French Toast Rounds, Egg Omelet, Bacon, Cheese) **(490 cal/25 g fat/2 g fiber)**
French Toast Sandwich w/Ham (French Toast Rounds, Egg Omelet, Ham, Cheese) **(470 cal/23 g fat/2 g fiber)**
Muffin - Blueberry **(420 cal/21 g fat/1 g fiber)**
SOURDOUGH Breakfast Sandwich w/Bacon (3 pc), Egg & Cheese **(380 cal/20 g fat/2 g fiber)**
SOURDOUGH Breakfast Sandwich w/Ham (2 sl), Egg & Cheese **(350 cal/18 g fat/2 g fiber)**

SOURDOUGH Breakfast Sandwich w/Sausage, Egg & Cheese **(500 cal/33 g fat/2 g fiber)**

Breakfast Platters

Biscuits (2) & Sausage Gravy Platter **(740 cal/40 g fat/2 g fiber)**

Pancake Platter (3 plain pancakes) **(240 cal/4 g fat/2 g fiber)**

Pancake Platter w/1 oz Breakfast Syrup **(330 cal/4 g fat/2 g fiber)**

Pancake Platter w/Sausage **(410 cal/19 g fat/2 g fiber)**

Pancake Platter w/Sausage & 1 oz Breakfast Syrup **(490 cal/19 g fat/2 g fiber)**

French Toast Kid's Meal (5 sticks, MOTT'S, 1% milk & syrup) **(660 cal/22 g fat/3 g fiber)**

French Toast Sticks Platter w/bacon & syrup packet **(530 cal/24 g fat/2 g fiber)**

French Toast Sticks Platter w/sausage & syrup packet **(640 cal/35 g fat/2 g fiber)**

Scrambled Egg Platter w/bacon (scrambled eggs, croissant, hashbrowns, bacon slices) **(670 cal/43 g fat/4 g fiber)**

Scrambled Egg Platter w/sausage (scrambled eggs, croissant, hashbrowns, sausage patty) **(790 cal/54 g fat/4 g fiber)**

Burgers & Sandwiches

Angus 'Shroom & Swiss **(710 cal/40 g fat/3 g fiber)**

Angus Cheesy Bacon Sandwich **(860 cal/51 g fat/2 g fiber)**

Texas WHOPPER **(820 cal/51 g fat/3 g fiber)**

Texas DOUBLE WHOPPER **(1050 cal/69 g fat/3 g fiber)**

Texas TRIPLE WHOPPER **(1290 cal/86 g fat/3 g fiber)**

Mustard WHOPPER **(560 cal/25 g fat/4 g fiber)**

Sourdough Bacon Cheeseburger (3.5 inch bun) **(640 cal/50 g fat/1 g fiber)**

Sourdough Bacon Cheeseburger (4.5 inch bun) **(670 cal/50 g fat/2 g fiber)**

Rodeo Cheeseburger **(380 cal/19 g fat/2 g fiber)**

CHICKEN TENDERS Sandwich **(440 cal/28 g fat/2 g fiber)**

Italian Chicken Sandwich **(560 cal/23 g fat/5 g fiber)**

TENDERCRISP Cheesy Bacon Sandwich **(870 cal/47 g fat/4 g fiber)**

Country Pork Sandwich **(700 cal/25 g fat/2 g fiber)**
Other Menu Items
Tacos (2) **(330 cal/23 g fat/5 g fiber)**
Mozzarella Sticks (4 pc) **(290 cal/16 g fat/0 g fiber)**
Marinara Sauce (1 oz) **(15 cal/0 g fat/0 g fiber)**
Chili (7.6 oz) **(190 cal/8 g fat/5 g fiber)**
Cheddar Cheese, Shredded (3/4 oz) **(90 cal/7 g fat/0 g fiber)**
Crackers (packet) **(25 cal/0.5 g fat/0 g fiber)**
French Fry Sauce (1 oz) **(90 cal/7 g fat/0 g fiber)**
Picante Sauce (0.5 oz) **(10 cal/0 g fat/0 g fiber)**
Iced Coffee
BK Mocha Joe Iced Coffee (22 fl oz) **(380 cal/10 g fat/1 g fiber)**
Desserts & Shakes
Dulce de Leche Pie **(280 cal/15 g fat/0 g fiber)**
Chocolate Chip Cookies (2) **(330 cal/15 g fat/1 g fiber)**
Oatmeal Raisin Cookies (2) **(310 cal/13 g fat/3 g fiber)**

Baskin-Robbins

Classic Flavors - 4 oz Scoop
Black Walnut Ice Cream **(280 cal/19 g fat/1 g fiber)**
Cherries Jubilee **(240 cal/12 g fat/1 g fiber)**
Chocolate Almond Ice Cream **(300 cal/18 g fat/1 g fiber)**
Chocolate Chip Cookie Dough Ice Cream **(290 cal/15 g fat/1 g fiber)**
Chocolate Chip Ice Cream **(270 cal/16 g fat/1 g fiber)**
Chocolate Fudge Ice Cream **(270 cal/15 g fat/0 g fiber)**
Chocolate Ice Cream **(260 cal/14 g fat/0 g fiber)**
Chocolate Oreao Cookie Ice cream **(330 cal/19 g fat/1 g fiber)**
Chocolate Ribbon Ice Cream **(240 cal/12 g fat/0 g fiber)**
French Vanilla Ice Cream **(280 cal/18 g fat/0 g fiber)**
Fudge Brownie Ice Cream **(300 cal/19 g fat/1 g fiber)**
German Chocolate Cake Ice Cream **(300 cal/16 g fat/1 g fiber)**
Gold Medal Ribbon Ice Cream **(260 cal/13 g fat/0 g fiber)**
Jamoca Almond Fudge Ice Cream **(270 cal/15 g fat/1 g fiber)**
Jamoca Ice Cream **(240 cal/13 g fat/0 g fiber)**
Mint Chocolate Chip Ice Cream **(270 cal/16 g fat/1 g fiber)**
Nutty Coconut Ice Cream **(300 cal/20 g fat/1 g fiber)**
Old Fashioned Butter Pecan Ice Cream **(280 cal/18 g fat/1 g fiber)**
Oreo Cookies 'n Cream Ice Cream **(280 cal/15 g fat/1 g fiber)**
Peanut Butter 'n Chocolate Ice Cream **(320 cal/20 g fat/1 g fiber)**
Pistachio Almond Ice Cream **(290 cal/19 g fat/1 g fiber)**
Pralines 'n Cream Ice Cream **(270 cal/14 g fat/0 g fiber)**
Reese's Peanut Butter Cup Ice Cream **(300 cal/18 g fat/0 g fiber)**
Rocky Road Ice Cream **(290 cal/15 g fat/1 g fiber)**
Vanilla Ice Cream **(260 cal/16 g fat/0 g fiber)**
Very Berry Strawberry Ice Cream **(220 cal/11 g fat/0 g**

fiber)
World Class Chocolate Ice Cream **(270 cal/15 g fat/0 g fiber)**

Seasonal - 4 oz Scoop
Banana Nut Ice Cream **(270 cal/15 g fat/0 g fiber)**
Bananas 'n Strawberries Ice Cream **(220 cal/9 g fat/0 g fiber)**
Baseball Nut Ice Cream **(270 cal/14 g fat/0 g fiber)**
Blueberry Cheesecake Ice Cream **(270 cal/14 g fat/0 g fiber)**
Candy Cookie Commotion Ice Cream **(300 cal/16 g fat/1 g fiber)**
Chocoholic's Resolution Ice Cream **(300 cal/16 g fat/0 g fiber)**
Chocolate Eclair Ice Cream **(300 cal/17 g fat/0 g fiber)**
Chocolate Mousse Crossing Ice Cream **(270 cal/15 g fat/0 g fiber)**
Chocolate Mousse Royale Ice Cream **(310 cal/16 g fat/1 g fiber)**
Cotton Candy Ice Cream **(260 cal/12 g fat/0 g fiber)**
Creme Brulee Ice Cream **(280 cal/11 g fat/0 g fiber)**
Creole Cheesecake Ice Cream **(240 cal/13 g fat/0 g fiber)**
Egg Nog Ice Cream **(250 cal/13 g fat/0 g fiber)**
Everyone's Favorite Candy Bar Ice Cream **(290 cal/14 g fat/0 g fiber)**
Happy Camper **(340 cal/22 g fat/2 g fiber)**
Honest to Goodnuts Ice Cream **(300 cal/14 g fat/0 g fiber)**
Hunka Chunka Chip Ice Cream **(300 cal/15 g fat/0 g fiber)**
Lemon Custard Ice Cream **(260 cal/13 g fat/0 g fiber)**
Love Potion #31 Ice Cream **(270 cal/14 g fat/1 g fiber)**
Macadamia Nuts 'n Cream Ice Cream **(290 cal/20 g fat/1 g fiber)**
Mississippi Mudd Ice Cream **(270 cal/13 g fat/1 g fiber)**
New York Cheesecake Ice Cream **(280 cal/16 g fat/0 g fiber)**
Oregon Blackberry Ice Cream **(240 cal/12 g fat/0 g fiber)**
Original Cinn Ice Cream **(290 cal/13 g fat/0 g fiber)**

Pink Bubblegum Ice Cream **(260 cal/12 g fat/0 g fiber)**
Pumpkin Pie Ice Cream **(230 cal/12 g fat/0 g fiber)**
Quarterback Crunch Ice Cream **(300 cal/17 g fat/0 g fiber)**
Strawberry Cheesecake Ice Cream **(270 cal/14 g fat/0 g fiber)**
Strawberry Shortcake Ice Cream **(280 cal/14 g fat/0 g fiber)**
Tax Crunch Ice Cream **(300 cal/18 g fat/1 g fiber)**
Tea of Tranquility **(270 cal/13 g fat/0 g fiber)**
Tiramisu Ice Cream **(260 cal/13 g fat/0 g fiber)**
Trick Oreo Treat Ice Cream **(300 cal/16 g fat/1 g fiber)**
True Blue Ginger Ice Cream **(270 cal/13 g fat/0 g fiber)**
Truffle In Paradise Ice Cream **(330 cal/21 g fat/1 g fiber)**
Turtle Cheesecake Ice Cream **(290 cal/16 g fat/1 g fiber)**
Winter White Chocolate Ice Cream **(270 cal/14 g fat/1 g fiber)**

Sundaes
2 Scoop Hot Fudge Sundae **(530 cal/29 g fat/0 g fiber)**
3 Scoop Hot Fudge Sundae **(750 cal/41 g fat/0 g fiber)**
Banana Royale **(630 cal/27 g fat/5 g fiber)**
Banana Split **(1030 cal/39 g fat/7 g fiber)**
Chocolate Bliss Sundae **(880 cal/42 g fat/5 g fiber)**
Happy Camper Waffle cone Sundae **(820 cal/41 g fat/5 g fiber)**
Peanut Butter Pie Sundae **(850 cal/59 g fat/5 g fiber)**
Tiramisu Sundae **(790 cal/39 g fat/1 g fiber)**

Bold Breeze
Kiwi Bold Breeze Large [32 fl.oz.] **(680 cal/1 g fat/5 g fiber)**
Kiwi Bold Breeze Medium [24 fl.oz.] **(470 cal/0.5 g fat/4 g fiber)** Kiwi Bold Breeze Small [16 fl.oz.] **(340 cal/0 g fat/3 g fiber)**
Mango Bold Breeze Large [32 fl.oz.] **(690 cal/2 g fat/3 g fiber)**
Mango Bold Breeze Medium [24 fl.oz.] **(470 cal/1.5 g fat/2 g fiber)**
Mango Bold Breeze Small [16 fl.oz.] **(340 cal/1 g fat/2 g fiber)**

Strawberry Citrus Bold Breeze Large [32 fl.oz.] **(700 cal/1.5 g fat/6 g fiber)**
Strawberry Citrus Bold Breeze Medium [24 fl.oz.] **(480 cal/1 g fat/4 g fiber)**
Strawberry Citrus Bold Breeze Small [16 fl.oz.] **(350 cal/1 g fat/3 g fiber)**
Creamy Bold Breeze
Kiwi Banana Creamy Bold Breeze Large [32 fl.oz.] **(960 cal/1.5 g fat/9 g fiber)**
Kiwi Banana Creamy Bold Breeze Medium [24 fl.oz.] **(710 cal/1.5 g fat/7 g fiber)**
Kiwi Banana Creamy Bold Breeze Small [16 fl.oz.] **(480 cal/1 g fat/4 g fiber)**
Kiwi Creamy Bold Breeze Medium [24 fl.oz.] **(620 cal/1 g fat/4 g fiber)**
Kiwi Creamy Bold Breeze Small [16 fl.oz.] **(440 cal/0.5 g fat/3 g fiber)**
Kiwi Pineapple Creamy Bold Breeze Large [32 fl.oz.] **(870 cal/1.5 g fat/6 g fiber)**
Mango Banana Creamy Bold Breeze Large [32 fl.oz.] **(970 cal/3 g fat/6 g fiber)**
Mango Banana Creamy Bold Breeze Medium [24 fl.oz.] **(720 cal/2.5 g fat/5 g fiber)**
Mango Banana Creamy Bold Breeze Small [16 fl.oz.] **(480 cal/1.5 g fat/3 g fiber)**
Strawberry Banana Creamy Bold Breeze Large [32 fl.oz.] **(980 cal/2.5 g fat/9 g fiber)**
Strawberry Banana Creamy Bold Breeze Medium [24 fl.oz.] **(730 cal/2 g fat/7 g fiber)**
Strawberry Banana Creamy Bold Breeze Small [16 fl.oz.] **(490 cal/1.5 g fat/5 g fiber)**
Strawberry Citrus Creamy Bold Breeze Large [32 fl.oz.] **(890 cal/2.5 g fat/6 g fiber)**
Strawberry Citrus Creamy Bold Breeze Medium [24 fl.oz.] **(630 cal/1.5 g fat/4 g fiber)**
Strawberry Citrus Creamy Bold Breeze Small [16 fl.oz.] **(450 cal/1 g fat/3 g fiber)**

Wild Mango Creamy Bold Breeze Large [32 fl.oz.] **(870 cal/3 g fat/4 g fiber)**
Wild Mango Creamy Bold Breeze Medium [24 fl.oz.] **(620 cal/2 g fat/3 g fiber)**
Wild Mango Creamy Bold Breeze Small [16 fl.oz.] **(440 cal/1.5 g fat/2 g fiber)**

Shakes

Chocolate Shake w/Chocolate Ice Cream Medium [24 fl.oz.] **(990 cal/40 g fat/1 g fiber)**
Chocolate Shake w/Chocolate Ice Cream Small [16 fl.oz.] **(620 cal/30 g fat/1 g fiber)**
Chocolate Shake w/Vanilla Ice Cream Medium [24 fl.oz.] **(1000 cal/45 g fat/0 g fiber)**
Chocolate Shake w/Vanilla Ice Cream Small [16 fl.oz.] **(690 cal/33 g fat/0 g fiber)**
Espresso Shake Medium [24 fl.oz.] **(790 cal/45 g fat/0 g fiber)**
Vanilla Shake Medium [24 fl.oz.] **(980 cal/45 g fat/0 g fiber)**
Vanilla Shake Small [16 fl.oz.] **(680 cal/33 g fat/0 g fiber)**

Cappuccino Blast

Brownie Blast Large [32 fl.oz.] **(1100 cal/42 g fat/5 g fiber)**
Brownie Blast Medium [24 fl.oz.] **(860 cal/33 g fat/4 g fiber)**
Brownie Blast Small [16 fl.oz.] **(580 cal/24 g fat/3 g fiber)**
Cappuccino Blast Large [32 fl.oz.] **(620 cal/24 g fat/0 g fiber)**
Cappuccino Blast w/Whipped Cream Large [32 fl.oz.] **(660 cal/28 g fat/0 g fiber)**
Cappuccino Blast Chocolate w/Whipped Cream Medium [24 fl.oz.] **(680 cal/19 g fat/0 g fiber)**
Cappuccino Blast Chocolate w/Whipped Cream Small [16 fl.oz.] **(450 cal/12 g fat/0 g fiber)**
Cappuccino Blast Low Fat Small [16 fl.oz.] **(220 cal/2 g fat/0 g fiber)**
Cappuccino Blast Medium [24 fl.oz.] **(460 cal/19 g fat/0 g fiber)**
Cappuccino Blast Mocha Large [32 fl.oz.] **(750 cal/23 g fat/0 g fiber)**

Cappuccino Blast Mocha Medium [24 fl.oz.] **(540 cal/18 g fat/0 g fiber)**
Cappuccino Blast Mocha Small [16 fl.oz.] **(380 cal/12 g fat/0 g fiber)**
Cappuccino Blast Mocha w/Whipped Cream Large [32 fl.oz.] **(790 cal/25 g fat/0 g fiber)**
Cappuccino Blast Mocha w/Whipped Cream Medium [24 fl.oz.] **(620 cal/21 g fat/0 g fiber)**
Cappuccino Blast Mocha w/Whipped Cream Small [16 fl.oz.] **(370 cal/13 g fat/0 g fiber)**
Cappuccino Blast Nonfat Small [16 fl.oz.] **(210 cal/0 g fat/0 g fiber)**
Cappuccino Blast Small [16 fl.oz.] **(300 cal/12 g fat/0 g fiber)**
Cappuccino Blast Turtle Large [32 fl.oz.] **(900 cal/28 g fat/1 g fibers)**
Cappuccino Blast Turtle Medium [24 fl.oz.] **(710 cal/23 g fat/0 g fiber)**
Cappuccino Blast Turtle Small [16 fl.oz.] **(480 cal/16 g fat/0 g fiber)**
Cappuccino Blast w/Whipped Cream Medium [24 fl.oz.] **(480 cal/21 g fat/0 g fiber)**
Cappuccino Blast w/Whipped Cream Small [16 fl.oz.] **(330 cal/14 g fat/0 g fiber)**
Nutty Smore's Blast Large [32 fl.oz.] **(1180 cal/40 g fat/2 g fiber)**
Nutty Smore's Blast Medium [24 fl.oz.] **(870 cal/32 g fat/2 g fiber)** Nutty Smore's Blast Small [16 fl.oz.] **(620 cal/23 g fat/1 g fiber)**
Oreo N'cookies Blast Large [32 fl.oz.] **(1030 cal/39 g fat/3 g fiber)**
Oreo N'cookies Blast Medium [24 fl.oz.] **(800 cal/31 g fat/2 g fiber)**
Oreo N'cookies Blast Small [16 fl.oz.] **(550 cal/22 g fat/2 g fiber)**

Ice Cream Cakes

Chocolate Chip Ice Cream/Devil's Food 9" Round Ice Cream

Cake [1 Serving (161 gm)] **(410 cal/23 g fat/2 g fiber)**
Oreo Cookies 'n Cream Ice Cream/Devil's Food 9" Round Ice Cream Cake [1 Serving (161 gm)] **(430 cal/23 g fat/1 g fiber)**
Pralines 'n Cream Ice Cream/Devil's Food 9" Round Ice Cream Cake [1 Serving (161 gm)] **(430 cal/20 g fat/1 g fiber)**
Chocolate Chip Ice Cream/Chocolate Roll Ice Cream Cake [1 Serving (117 gm)] **(290 cal/15 g fat/2 g fiber)**
Mint Chocolate Chip Ice Cream/Chocolate Roll Ice Cream Cake [1 Serving (117 gm)] **(290 cal/14 g fat/2 g fiber)**
Vanilla Ice Cream/Chocolate Roll Ice Cream Cake [1 Serving (117 gm)] **(270 cal/14 g fat/2 g fiber)**
Chocolate Chip Ice Cream/Devil's Food Sheet Ice Cream Cake [1 Serving (125 gm)] **(330 cal/18 g fat/1 g fiber)**
Mint Chocolate Chip Ice Cream/Devil's Food Sheet Ice Cream Cake [1 Serving (113 gm)] **(290 cal/18 g fat/1 g fiber)**
Oreo Cookies 'n Cream Ice Cream/White Sponge Sheet Ice Cream Cake [1 Serving (113 gm)] **(300 cal/14 g fat/1 g fiber)**
Pralines 'n Cream Ice Cream/White Sponge Sheet Ice Cream Cake [1 Serving (113 gm)] **(300 cal/16 g fat/1 g fiber)**
Vanilla Ice Cream/Devil's Food Sheet Ice Cream Cake [1 Serving (113 gm)] **(300 cal/19 g fat/1 g fiber)**
Chocolate Chip Ice Cream/Devil's Food Heart Ice Cream Cake [1 Serving (125 gm)] **(330 cal/18 g fat/1 g fiber)**
Oreo Cookies 'n Cream Heart Ice Cream Cake [1 Serving (125 gm)] **(300 cal/16 g fat/1 g fiber)**
Oreo Cookies 'n Cream Ice Cream/Devil's Food Heart Ice Cream Cake [1 Serving (125 gm)] **(330 cal/17 g fat/1 g fiber)**
Vanilla Ice Cream Heart Ice Cream Cake [1 Serving (125 gm)] **(290 cal/18 g fat/0 g fiber)**
Vanilla Ice Cream/Devil's Food Heart Ice Cream Cake [1 Serving (125 gm)] **(340 cal/19 g fat/1 g fiber)**
Low Fat Ice Cream - 4 oz Scoop
Espresso 'n Cream Low Fat Ice Cream **(180 cal/4 g fat/1 g fiber)**
Sugar Free Non Fat Ice Cream
Berries 'n Banana No Sugar Added Low Fat Ice Cream **(110 cal/2 g fat/1 g fiber)**

Blueberry Swirl Ice Cream **(130 cal/2 g fat/1 g fiber)**
Caramel Turtle No Sugar Added Low Fat Ice Cream **(160 cal/4 g fat/0 g fiber)**
Chocolate Chip No Sugar Added Low Fat Ice Cream **(170 cal/4.5 g fat/1 g fiber)**
Chocolate Chocolate Chip No Sugar Added Low Fat Ice Cream **(150 cal/4.5 g fat/1 g fiber)**
Chocolate Cookie No Sugar Added Low Fat Ice Cream **(160 cal/5 g fat/1 g fiber)**
Mad About Chocolate NSA Lowfat Ice Cream **(160 cal/5 g fat/1 g fiber)**
Pineapple Coconut No Sugar Added Low Fat Ice Cream **(150 cal/2 g fat/0 g fiber)**
Tin Roof Sundae No Sugar Added Low Fat Ice Cream **(190 cal/3 g fat/1 g fiber)**
Low Fat / Non Fat Yogurt - 4 oz Scoop
Maui Brownie Madness Low Fat Yogurt **(210 cal/4 g fat/2 g fiber)**
Perils of Praline Low Fat Yogurt **(190 cal/3.5 g fat/1 g fiber)**
Vanilla Nonfat Yogurt **(150 cal/0 g fat/0 g fiber)**
Non Fat Soft Yogurt - 1/2 cup
Chocolate Nonfat Soft Serve Yogurt **(120 cal/0 g fat/1 g fiber)**
Peppermint Nonfat Soft Serve Yogurt **(110 cal/0 g fat/0 g fiber)**
Red Raspberry Nonfat Soft Serve Yogurt **(110 cal/0 g fat/0g fiber)**
Vanilla Nonfat SoftServe Yogurt **(110 cal/0 g fat/0 g fiber)**
Sugar Free Non Fat Soft Yogurt - 1/2 cup
Truly Free Butter Pecan No Sugar Added Nonfat Soft Serve Yogurt **(90 cal/0 g fat/1 g fiber)**
Truly Free Cafe Mocha Nonfat Soft Serve Yogurt **(90 cal/0 g fat/1 g fiber)**
Truly Free Chocolate No Sugar Added Nonfat Soft Serve Yogurt **(80 cal/0 g fat/0 g fiber)**
Truly Free Strawberry Patch No Sugar Nonfat Soft Serve Yogurt **(90 cal/0 g fat/1 g fiber)**

Truly Free Vanilla No Sugar Added Nonfat Soft Serve Yogurt
(90 cal/0 g fat/1 g fiber)
Sherbet - 4 oz Scoop
Blue Raspberry Sherbet (160 cal/2 g fat/0 g fiber)
Orange Sherbet (160 cal/2 g fat/0 g fiber)
Rainbow Sherbet (160 cal/2 g fat/0 g fiber)
Red Raspberry Sherbet (160 cal/2 g fat/0 g fiber)
Rock 'n Pop Swirl Sherbet (190 cal/4 g fat/0 g fiber)
Twisted Chip Sherbet (180 cal/3 g fat/0 g fiber)
Wild 'N Reckless Spirit Sherbet (160 cal/2 g fat/0 g fiber)
Ices - 4 oz Scoop
Daiquiri Ice (130 cal/0 g fat/0 g fiber)
Margarita Ice (130 cal/0 g fat/0 g fiber)
Pineapple Ice/Sorbet (140 cal/0 g fat/0 g fiber)
Watermelon Ice (130 cal/0 g fat/0 g fiber)

Cheesecake Factory

Asian Chicken Salad **(574 cal/31 g fat)**
Spicy Chicken Salad **(490 cal/14 g fat)**
Pear Endive Salad **(500 cal/23 g fat)**
California Salad **(560 cal/28 g fat)**
Salmon Seafood Salad **(566 cal/35 g fat)**
Tuna Seafood Salad **(520 cal/22 g fat)**
Other Menu Items
Luau Salad (4 servings) **(801 cal/31.9 g fat/10.6 g fiber)**
Cheesecake (per slice)
6 Carb Cheesecake (1 slice, no whipped cream or berries) **(610 cal/29 g fat/0 g fiber)**
Brownie Sundae Cheesecake **(960 cal/62 g fat)**
Chocolate Chip Cookie Dough Cheesecake (1 slice) **(1090 cal/72 g fat/3 g fiber)**
Dulce de Leche Caramel Cheesecake **(1010 cal/71 g fat)**
Fresh Banana Cream Cheesecake **(860 cal/61 g fat)**
Keylime Cheesecake **(710 cal/49 g fat)**
Low Carb Cheesecake **(w/Splenda) (420 cal/38g fat/12g fiber)**
Original Cheesecake **(640 cal/45 g fat)**
Plain Cheesecake (1 slice) **(315 cal/20 g fat/0 g fiber)**
Snicker's Cheesecake (1 slice) **(920 cal/63 g fat/2 g fiber)**
Vanilla Bean Cheesecake **(870 cal/62 g fat)**
White Chocolate Raspberry Truffle **(910 cal/61 g fat)**

Country Buffet/Hometown Buffet/Old Country Buffet

Breads
Biscuits [1 biscuit] **(180 cal/7 g fat/1 g fiber)**
Breadsticks [1 breadstick/47g] **(140 cal/4.5 g fat/0 g fiber)**
Buns: Hot Dog [1 bun/43g] **(120 cal/2 g fat/1 g fiber)**
Buns: Sandwich [1 bun/43g] **(120 cal/2 g fat/1 g fiber)**
Cinnamon Bread [1 slice/50g] **(45 cal/0.5 g fat/0 g fiber)**
Cinnamon Sugared Donut Holes [1 piece/11g] **(50 cal/3g fat/0g fiber)**
Dinner Rolls: Wheat [1 roll/36g] **(110 cal/3 g fat/1 g fiber)**
Dinner Rolls: White [1 roll/36g] **(120 cal/3.5 g fat/1 g fiber)**
English Muffin [1/2 muffin/26g] **(60 cal/0.5 g fat/0 g fiber)**
Flour Tortilla [1 tortilla/38g] **(120 cal/3 g fat/1 g fiber)**
French Toast [1 slice/74g] **(170 cal/8 g fat/0 g fiber)**
Glazed Donuts [1 donut/34g] **(130 cal/7 g fat/0 g fiber)**
Pancakes [1 pancake/49g] **(120 cal/3.5 g fat/0 g fiber)**
Taco Shells [1 shell/11g] **(50 cal/2.5 g fat/0 g fiber)**
Waffles [1 waffle/41g] **(120 cal/3 g fat/0 g fiber)**

Condiments
Bacon Bits: real [1 spoon/7g] **(25 cal/1.5 g fat/0 g fiber)**
Black Olives: sliced [1 spoon/15g] **(15 cal/1.5 g fat/0 g fiber)**
Blueberry Syrup [2 fl oz ladle/71g] **(250 cal/0 g fat/0 g fiber)**
Brown Sugar [1 tbsp/9g] **(35 cal/0 g fat/0 g fiber)**
Butter: packet [1 packet/5g] **(35 cal/4 g fat/0 g fiber)**
Cheese: Shredded Cheddar [1 spoon/10g] **(40 cal/3.5 g fat0 fiber)**
Cheese: Grated Parmesan [1 spoon/7g] **(30 cal/2 g fat/0 g fiber)**
Cherry Peppers [1 spoon/11g] **(4 cal/0 g fat/0 g fiber)**
Cocktail Sauce [1 ladle/30g] **(30 cal/0 g fat/0 g fiber)**
Coffee Creamers: packet [1 packet/11g] **(15 cal/1 g fat/0 g fiber)**
Cranberry Sauce [1 ladle/30g] **(45 cal/0 g fat/0 g fiber)**
Creamy Cheese Sauce [1 ladle/62g] **(50 cal/1.5 g fat/0 g fiber)**

Crushed Red Pepper [1 tsp/2g] **(10 cal/0.5 g fat/0 g fiber)**
Diced Onions [1 spoon/15g] **(5 cal/0 g fat/0 g fiber)**
Hollandaise Sauce [2 fl oz ladle/50g] **(130 cal/13 g fat/0 g fiber)**
Honey: packet [1 packet/14g] **(45 cal/0 g fat/0 g fiber)**
Horseradish Sauce [1 ladle/30g] **(60 cal/5 g fat/0 g fiber)**
Hot Sauce [1 tsp/5g] **(0 cal/0 g fat/0 g fiber)**
Jalapeno Peppers [1 spoon/11g] **(2 cal/0 g fat/0 g fiber)**
Jelly: packet [1 packet/14g] **(35 cal/0 g fat/0 g fiber)**
Ketchup [1 tbsp/15g] **(15 cal/0 g fat/0 g fiber)**
Lemons [1 slice/8g] **(2 cal/0 g fat/0 g fiber)**
Lettuce: shredded [1/4 cup/14g] **(0 cal/0 g fat/0 g fiber)**
Maple Syrup [2 fl oz ladle/68g] **(180 cal/0 g fat/0 g fiber)**
Margarine: melted [2 fl oz ladle/56g] **(410 cal/45 g fat/0 g fiber)**
Margarine: packet [1 packet/5g] **(25 cal/3 g fat/0 g fiber)**
Mayonnaise [1 tbsp/14g] **(100 cal/11 g fat/0 g fiber)**
Mustard [1 tbsp/15g] **(10 cal/0.5 g fat/0 g fiber)**
Non-Dairy Creamers: packet [1 packet/11g] **(10 cal/0.5 g fat/0 g fiber)**
Peanut Butter [1 tbsp/16g] **(100 cal/8 g fat/1 g fiber)**
Pepperoncini Peppers [1 spoon/11g] **(2 cal/0 g fat/0 g fiber)**
Salsa [1 ladle/30g] **(10 cal/0 g fat/0 g fiber)**
Sauteed Green Peppers [1 spoon/54g] **(25 cal/1.5 g fat/0 g fiber)**
Sauteed Mushrooms [1 spoon/51g] **(30 cal/2.5 g fat/0 g fiber)**
Sauteed Onions [1 spoon/51g] **(30 cal/1 g fat/0 g fiber)**
Shredded Lettuce [1/4 cup/11g] **(0 cal/0 g fat/0 g fiber)**
Sliced Pickles [1 spoon/11g] **(2 cal/0 g fat/0 g fiber)**
Sliced/Diced Tomatoes [1 spoon/15g] **(2 cal/0 g fat/0 g fiber)**
Sour Cream [1 spoon/12g] **(25 cal/2.5 g fat/0 g fiber)**
Soy Sauce [1 tsp/5g] **(2 cal/0 g fat/0 g fiber)**
Sweet Pickle Relish [1 tbsp/15g] **(25 cal/0 g fat/0 g fiber)**
Tabasco Sauce [1 tsp/5g] **(0 cal/0 g fat/0 g fiber)**
Desserts

Apple Crisp [1 spoon/94g] **(150 cal/3.5 g fat/2 g fiber)**
Apple Pie-Reduced Sugar [1 piece/116g] **(190 cal/11 g fat 4g fiber)**
Apple Strudel Bites [1 piece/60g] **(90 cal/6 g fat/0 g fiber)**
Bread Pudding [1 spoon/96g] **(190 cal/8 g fat/0 g fiber)**
Butterfinger Pieces [1 spoon/15g] **(70 cal/2.5 g fat/0 g fiber)**
Butterscotch Topping [1 pump/75g] **(230 cal/1 g fat/0 g fiber)**
Cheesecake: plain [1 piece/80g] **(220 cal/10 g fat/0 g fiber)**
Chocolate Chips [1 spoon/15g] **(90 cal/5 g fat/0 g fiber)**
Chocolate Cream Pie-Reduced Sugar [1 piece/79g] **(190 cal/12 g fat/0 g fiber)**
Chocolate Decadence Cake [1 piece/64g] **(200 cal/9 g fat/0 g fiber)**
Chocolate Syrup [1 pump/37g] **(80 cal/0 g fat/0 g fiber)**
Cone: Ice Cream [1 cone/4g] **(15 cal/0 g fat/0 g fiber)**
Cookie-Sugar Free Ranger [1 cookie/20g] **(100 cal/5 g fat/0 g fiber)**
FunE Chips [1 spoon/15g] **(80 cal/3 g fat/0 g fiber)**
Gummy Bears [9 pieces/20g] **(60 cal/0 g fat/0 g fiber)**
Honey Nut Topping [1 spoon/28g] **(150 cal/12 g fat/2 g fiber)**
Hot Fudge Sundae Cake [1 spoon/86g] **(160 cal/3.5 g fat/0 g fiber)**
Hot Fudge Topping [1 pump/41g] **(120 cal/3 g fat/0 g fiber)**
Hydrox Cookies: Crushed [1 spoon/8g] **(35 cal/1.5 g fat/0 g fiber)**
Malted Milk Balls: Ground [1 spoon/15g] **(70 cal/3 g fat/0 g fiber)**
Nestle Crunch Pieces [1 spoon/15g] **(80 cal/4 g fat/0 g fiber)**
Pudding: Chocolate [1 spoon/86g] **(150 cal/7 g fat/0 g fiber)**
Pudding: Chocolate/Reduced Sugar/Calorie [1 spoon/86g] **(70 cal/1 g fat/0 g fiber)**
Pudding: Vanilla [1 spoon/86g] **(140 cal/6 g fat/0 g fiber)**
Pudding: Vanilla/Reduced Sugar/Calorie [1 spoon/86g] **(70 cal/1 g fat/0 g fiber)**

Pumpkin Pie [1 piece/119g] **(270 cal/9 g fat/2 g fiber)**
Rainbow Sprinkles [1 spoon/15g] **(70 cal/2 g fat/0 g fiber)**
Reduced Sugar Pie-Cherry [1 piece/95g] **(160 cal/9 g fat/0 g fiber)**
Reduced Sugar Pie-Lemon [1 piece/95g] **(160 cal/9 g fat/0 g fiber)**
Reduced Sugar Pie-Lime [1 piece/95g] **(160 cal/9 g fat/0 g fiber)**
Reduced Sugar Pie-Orange [1 piece/95g] **(160 cal/9 g fat/0 g fiber)**
Reduced Sugar Pie-Raspberry [1 piece/95g] **(160 cal/9g fat/0g fiber)**
Reduced Sugar Pie-Strawberry [1 piece/95g] **(160 cal/9g fat/0g fiber)**
Soft Serve Frozen Yogurt: Nonfat/Strawberry [4 fl. oz./88g] **(100 cal/0 g fat/0 g fiber)**
Soft Serve Frozen Yogurt: Nonfat/Vanilla [4 fl. oz./89g] **(110 cal/0 g fat/0 g fiber)**
Soft Serve: Chocolate [4 fl. oz./113g] **(140 cal/4.5 g fat/0 g fiber)**
Soft Serve: Vanilla [4 fl. oz./113g] **(150 cal/5 g fat/0 g fiber)**
Soft Serve Frozen Yogurt: Nonfat/Nutrasweet/Vanilla [4 fl. oz./87g] **(80 cal/0 g fat/0 g fiber)**
Strawberry Topping [1 pump/47g] **(100 cal/0 g fat/0 g fiber)**
Whipped Topping: Non Dairy [1 spoon/21g] **(60 cal/4.5 g fat/0 g fiber)**

Dressings

Bleu Cheese Dressing [1 ladle/30g] **(170 cal/18 g fat/0 g fiber)**
Creamy Italian Dressing [1 ladle/29g] **(110 cal/11 g fat/0 g fiber)**
Fat Free French Dressing [1 ladle/30g] **(35 cal/0 g fat/0 g fiber)**
French Dressing [1 ladle/33g] **(150 cal/12 g fat/0 g fiber)**
Italian Dressing [1 ladle/32g] **(120 cal/11 g fat/0 g fiber)**
Low Fat Italian Dressing [1 ladle/30g] **(25 cal/2 g fat/0 g**

Honeydew [1 spoon/88g] **(30 cal/0 g fat/0 g fiber)**
Pineapple [1 spoon/78g] **(35 cal/0 g fat/1 g fiber)**
Strawberries [1 spoon/72g] **(25 cal/0 g fat/1 g fiber)**
Watermelon [1 spoon/76g] **(25 cal/0 g fat/0 g fiber)**

Gravies & Sauces

Au Jus [2 fl. oz ladle/55g] **(0 cal/0 g fat/0 g fiber)**
Gravy: Beef [2 fl oz ladle/55g] **(30 cal/2 g fat/0 g fiber)**
Gravy: Chicken [2 fl oz ladle/55g] **(30 cal/1 g fat/0 g fiber)**
Gravy: Country [2 fl. oz ladle/55g] **(120 cal/8 g fat/0 g fiber)**
Gravy: Roasted Pork [2 fl oz ladle/55g] **(50 cal/4 g fat/0 g fiber)**
Gravy: Turkey [2 fl. oz ladle/55g] **(10 cal/0 g fat/0 g fiber)**
Meat Sauce [2 fl oz ladle/107g] **(70 cal/3 g fat/0 g fiber)**

Salads

Ambrosia [1 spoon/89g] **(140 cal/5 g fat/1 g fiber)**
BLT Salad [1 spoon/70g] **(150 cal/14 g fat/0 g fiber)**
Broccoli Apple Salad [1 spoon/100g] **(160 cal/11 g fat/2 g fiber)**
Caesar Salad [1 cup/65g] **(80 cal/6 g fat/1 g fiber)**
California Coleslaw [1 spoon/100g] **(90 cal/0.5 g fat/1 g fiber)**
Carrot & Raisin Salad [1 spoon/100g] **(140 cal/8 g fat/2 g fiber)**
Chicken Pasta Salad [1 spoon/100g] **(230 cal/18 g fat/1 g fiber)**
Creamy Pea Salad [1 spoon/100g] **(160 cal/11 g fat/4 g fiber)**
Cucumber Tomato Salad [1 spoon/100g] **(30 cal/1 g fat/1 g fiber)**
Dilled Potato Salad [1 spoon/83g] **(110 cal/8 g fat/1 g fiber)**
Flavored Gelatin [1 spoon/70g] **(40 cal/0 g fat/0 g fiber)**
Gelatin Whip [1 spoon/68g] **(80 cal/2.5 g fat/0 g fiber)**
Greek Salad [1 spoon/75g] **(120 cal/8 g fat/1 g fiber)**
Macaroni Vegetable Salad [1 spoon/100g] **(230 cal/15 g fat/1 g fiber)**
Marinated Vegetables [1 spoon/100g] **(60 cal/3.5 g fat/1 g**

fiber)
Oriental Pasta [1 spoon/100g] **(110 cal/6 g fat/2 g fiber)**
Pickled Beets [1 spoon/100g] **(100 cal/0 g fat/2 g fiber)**
Potato Salad [1 spoon/75g] **(110 cal/5 g fat/1 g fiber)**
Prunes: Stewed [1 spoon/71g] **(100 cal/0 g fat/2 g fiber)**
Raisin Fluff [1 spoon/80g] **(140 cal/4 g fat/0 g fiber)**
Seafood Salad [1 spoon/117g] **(310 cal/26 g fat/1 g fiber)**
Seven Layer Salad [1 spoon/75g] **(180 cal/17 g fat/1 g fibers)**
Sicilian Pasta Salad [1 spoon/100g] **(150 cal/9 g fat/2 g fiber)**
Spring Mix [1 cup/45g] **(5 cal/0 g fat/1 g fiber)**
Strawberry-Banana Salad [1 spoon/85g] **(70 cal/0.5 g fat/2 g fiber)**
Strawberry-Peach-Banana [1 spoon/79g] **(80 cal/1 g fat/1 g fiber)**
Strawberry Whip [1 spoon/76g] **(200 cal/14 g fat/0 g fiber)**
Tarragon Potato Salad [1 spoon/82g] **(120 cal/7 g fat/1 g fiber)**
Three Bean Salad [1 spoon/100g] **(90 cal/4.5 g fat/3 g fiber)**
Tossed Green Salad [1 cup/45g] **(5 cal/0 g fat/1 g fiber)**
Waldorf Salad [1 spoon/60g] **(110 cal/7 g fat/1 g fiber)**
Whipped Pineapple/Banana [1 spoon/114g] **(180 cal/1.5 g fat/0 g fiber)**

Salad Toppers
Bacon Bits: Imitation [1 spoon/7g] **(30 cal/1 g fat/0 g fiber)**
Black Olives: sliced [1 spoon/15g] **(15 cal/1.5 g fat/0 g fiber)**
Carrots: julienne [1 spoon/8g] **(5 cal/5 g fat/0 g fiber)**
Cherry Tomatoes [1 item/17g] **(5 cal/0 g fat/0 g fiber)**
Chow Mein Noodles [1 spoon/7g] **(35 cal/1.5 g fat/0 g fiber)**
Croutons [7 croutons/7g] **(35 cal/1.5 g fat/0 g fiber)**
Cucumbers: sliced [1 slice/15g] **(2 cal/0 g fat/0 g fiber)**
Eggs: hard cooked/diced [1 spoon/15g] **(20 cal/1.5 g fat 0g fiber)**
Feta Cheese [1 spoon/40g] **(35 cal/3 g fat/0 g fiber)**
Mushrooms: sliced [1 spoon/10g] **(2 cal/0 g fat/0 g fiber)**
Parmesan Cheese: grated [1 spoon/7g] **(30 cal/2 g fat/0 g**

fiber)
Peas [1 spoon/15g] (10 cal/0 g fat/1 g fiber)
Pepperoncini [1 spoon/11g] (2 cal/0 g fat/0 g fiber)
Raisins [1 spoon/12g] (40 cal/0 g fat/0 g fiber)
Red Onions: sliced [1 ring/6g] (2 cal/0 g fat/0 g fiber)
Shredded Cheese: Imitation [1 spoon/10g] (25 cal/2 g fat/0 g fiber)
Spinach Leaves [1 cup/32g] (5 cal/0 g fat/0 g fiber)
Sunflower seeds [1 spoon/11g] (70 cal/6 g fat/0 g fiber)

Sides

Bacon [1 slice/6g] (30 cal/2.5 g fat/0 g fiber)
Baked Beans [1 spoon/110g] (120 cal/0.5 g fat/4 g fiber)
Bread Dressing [1 spoon/100g] (130 cal/3.5 g fat/1 g fiber)
Cabbage: German Boiled [1 spoon/85g] (40 cal/3.5 g fat/1 g fiber)
Cabbage: Green [1 spoon/85g] (40 cal/3 g fat/1 g fiber)
Carrots: steamed [1 spoon/85g] (40 cal/0 g fat/3 g fiber)
Chesapeake Corn [1 spoon/85g] (80 cal/3 g fat/2 g fiber)
Corn on the Cob [1 piece/72g] (100 cal/3 g fat/1 g fiber)
Corn: steamed [1 spoon/85g] (100 cal/1 g fat/2 g fiber)
Creamy Cheese Sauce [2 fl oz ladle/62g] (50 cal/1.5 g fat/0 g fiber)
French Fries [22 fries/51g] (190 cal/9 g fat/2 g fiber)
Fried Rice w/Ham [1 spoon/100g] (170 cal/6 g fat/1 g fiber)
Green Bean Casserole [1 spoon/110g] (60 cal/3 g fat/2 g fiber)
Green Beans [1 spoon/85g] (15 cal/0 g fat/1 g fiber)
Green Beans El Greco [1 spoon/85g] (20 cal/0 g fat/2 g fiber)
Grits [4 fl oz ladle/121g] (70 cal/0 g fat/0 g fiber)
Italian Style Green Beans w/Bacon [1 spoon/85g] (60 cal/4 g fat/2 g fiber)
Joe's Cracked Pepper Green Beans w [1 spoon/85g] (70 cal/6 g fat/2 g fiber)
Montreal Vegetable Medley [1 spoon/85g] (40 cal/3.5 g fat/1 g fiber)
Oatmeal [4 fl oz ladle/117g] (70 cal/1 g fat/2 g fiber)

Pinto Beans w/Ham [1 spoon/85g] **(90 cal/1 g fat/7 g fiber)**
Potatoes: Baked [1 each/180g] **(160 cal/0 g fat/3 g fiber)**
Potatoes: Baked Sweet [1 each/192g] **(160 cal/0 g fat/6 g fiber)**
Potatoes: Hash Browns [1 spoon/80g] **(110 cal/6 g fat/1 g fiber)**
Potatoes: Hash Brown Patties [1 pattie/57g] **(120 cal/8 g fat/1 g fiber)**
Potatoes: Jo Jo [6-7 pieces/84g] **(210 cal/15 g fat/2 g fiber)**
Potatoes: O'Brien [1 spoon/110g] **(120 cal/6 g fat/2 g fiber)**
Potatoes: Red [1 spoon/113g] **(100 cal/3 g fat/2 g fiber)**
Red Beans w/Ham [1 spoon/85g] **(90 cal/1 g fat/7 g fiber)**
Sausage Links [1 link/25g] **(100 cal/10 g fat/0 g fiber)**
Spaghetti [1 spoon/85g] **(90 cal/0.5 g fat/1 g fiber)**
Spinach Marie [1 spoon/110g] **(210 cal/17 g fat/1 g fiber)**
Squash: winter [1 spoon/85g] **(150 cal/9 g fat/1 g fiber)**
Turnip or Collard Greens w/Bacon [1 spoon/110g] **(40 cal/3 g fat/1 g fiber)**
Vegetable Stir Fry [1 spoon/85g] **(25 cal/0.5 g fat/2 g fiber)**
White Rice [1 spoon/100g] **(90 cal/0 g fat/0 g fiber)**
Wild Rice Vegetable Pilaf [1 spoon/100g] **(90 cal/1 g fat/0 g fiber)**
Yams: Candied [1 spoon/118g] **(140 cal/1.5 g fat/1 g fiber)**
Zucchini: Sauteed [1 spoon/85g] **(50 cal/4 g fat/1 g fiber)**
Soups
Chicken Noodle Soup [4 fl oz ladle/123g] **(70 cal/2 g fat/0 g fibers)** Chicken Rice Soup [4 fl oz ladle/123g] **(70 cal/1.5 g fat/0 g fiber)**
Chili Bean Soup [4 fl oz ladle/123g] **(100 cal/3.5 g fat/1 g fiber)**
Corn Chowder [4 fl oz ladle/123g] **(140 cal/8 g fat/1 g fiber)**
Cream of Broccoli Soup [4 fl oz ladle/123g] **(80 cal/7 g fat/1 g fiber)**
Navy Bean Soup w/Ham [4 fl oz ladle/123g] **(50 cal/1 g fat/4 g fiber)**

New England Clam Chowder [4 fl oz ladle/123g] **(300 cal/12 g fat/0 g fiber)**
Potato Cheese Soup [4 fl oz ladle/123g] **(130 cal/9 g fat/1 g fiber)**

Dominoes

Sides
Breadsticks [1 of 8 average-sized sticks] **(130 cal/7 g fat/1 g fiber)** Cheesy Bread [1 of 8 average-sized sticks] **(140 cal/7 g fat/1 g fiber)**
Cinna Stix [1 of 8 average-sized sticks] **(140 cal/7 g fat/1 g fiber)**
Marinara Dipping Sauce [1 container] **(25 cal/0 g fat/1 g fiber)**
Garlic Dipping Sauce [1 container] **(440 cal/50 g fat/0 g fiber)**
Sweet Icing Dipping Sauce [1 container] **(250 cal/3 g fat/0 g fiber)**
Domino's Pizza Chicken Kickers [1] **(45 cal/2 g fat/0 g fiber)**
Barbeque Buffalo Wings [1] **(88 cal/4.5 g fat/0 g fiber)**
Hot Buffalo Wings [1] **(85 cal/4.5 g fat/0 g fiber)**
Hot Dipping Sauce [1 container] **(120 cal/12 g fat/0 g fiber)**
Ranch Dipping Sauce [1 container] **(200 cal/21 g fat/0 g fiber)**
Blue Cheese Dipping Sauce [1 container] **(230 cal/24 g fat/0 g fiber)**
Garden Fresh Salad [1/2 order] **(70 cal/4 g fat/1 g fiber)**
Grilled Chicken Caesar Salad [1/2 order] **(105 cal/4 g fat/1 g fiber)**
Blue Cheese Dressing [1 package] **(230 cal/24 g fat/0 g fiber)**
Buttermilk Ranch Dressing [1 package] **(220 cal/24 g fat/0 g fiber)**
Creamy Caesar Dressing [1 package] **(210 cal/22 g fat/0 g fiber)**
Golden Italian Dressing [1 package] **(220 cal/23 g fat/0 g fiber)**
Light Italian Dressing [1 package] **(20 cal/0 g fat/0 g fiber)**
Toppings for Medium Pizza - 1/8th of pizza - add to cheese pizza to get total
Classic Hand-Tossed Crust for Medium Pizza **(160 cal/3 g**

fat/1 g fiber)
Ultimate Deep Dish Crust for Medium Pizza (160 cal/6 g fat/3 g fiber)
Crunchy Thin Crust for Medium Pizza (80 cal/3.5 g fat/1 g fiber)
Pizza Sauce for Medium Pizza (10 cal/1 g fat/0 g fiber)
Hand-Tossed & Thin Crust Cheese for Medium Pizza (45 cal/4 g fat/0 g fiber)
Deep Dish Cheese for Medium Pizza (60 cal/5 g fat/0 g fiber)
Extra Cheese for Medium Pizza (25 cal/2 g fat/0 g fiber)
Pepperoni Topping for Topping for Medium Pizza (40 cal/3.5 g fat/0 g fiber)
Ham Topping for Medium Pizza (10 cal/0 g fat/0 g fiber)
Sausage Topping for Medium Pizza (30 cal/2.5 g fat/0 g fiber)
Beef Topping for Medium Pizza (25 cal/2.5 g fat/0 g fiber)
Onions Topping for Medium Pizza (0 cal/0 g fat/0 g fiber)
Green Pepper Topping for Medium Pizza (0 cal/0 g fat/0 g fiber)
Mushrooms Topping for Medium Pizza (0 cal/0 g fat/0 g fiber)
Ripe (Black) Olives Topping for Medium Pizza (5 cal/1 g fat/0 g fiber)
Pineapple Topping for Medium Pizza (5 cal/0 g fat/0 g fiber)
American Cheese Topping for Medium Pizza (40 cal/3 g fat/0 g fiber)
Cheddar Cheese Topping for Medium Pizza (30 cal/2.5 g fat/0 g fiber)
Provolone Cheese Topping for Medium Pizza (45 cal/3.5 g fat/0 g fiber)
Anchovies Topping for Medium Pizza (0 cal/0 g fat/0 g fiber)
Bacon Topping for Medium Pizza (25 cal/2 g fat/0 g fiber)
Grilled Chicken Topping for Medium Pizza (15 cal/0 g fat/0 g fiber)
Philly Steak Topping for Medium Pizza (10 cal/0 g fat/0 g fiber)

Banana Peppers Topping for Medium Pizza **(0 cal/0 g fat/0 g fiber)**
Green Chile Peppers Topping for Medium Pizza **(0 cal/0 g fat/0 g fiber)**
Green Olives Topping for Medium Pizza **(10 cal/1 g fat/0 g fiber)**
Garlic Topping for Medium Pizza **(10 cal/0 g fat/0 g fiber)**
Jalapeno Peppers Topping for Medium Pizza **(0 cal/0 g fat/0 g fiber)**
Tomatoes Topping for Medium Pizza **(0 cal/0 g fat/0 g fiber)**
Toppings for Large Pizza - 1/8th of pizza - add to cheese pizza to get total
Classic Hand-Tossed Crust for Large Pizza **(220 cal/4 g fat/2 g fiber)**
Ultimate Deep Dish Crust for Large Pizza **(230 cal/7 g fat/4 g fiber)**
Crunchy Thin Crust for Large Pizza **(110 cal/4.5 g fat/1 g fiber)**
Pizza Sauce for Large Pizza **(10 cal/0 g fat/1 g fiber)**
Hand-Tossed & Thin Crust Cheese for Large Pizza **(60 cal/5 g fat/0 g fiber)**
Deep Dish Cheese for Large Pizza **(80 cal/7 g fat/0 g fiber)**
Extra Cheese for Large Pizza **(30 cal/2.5 g fat/0 g fiber)**
Pepperoni Topping for Topping for Large Pizza **(50 cal/4.5 g fat/0 g fiber)**
Ham Topping for Large Pizza **(15 cal/0.5 g fat/0 g fiber)**
Sausage Topping for Large Pizza **(60 cal/5.5 g fat/1 g fiber)**
Beef Topping for Large Pizza **(50 cal/4.5 g fat/0 g fiber)**
Onions Topping for Large Pizza **(0 cal/0 g fat/0 g fiber)**
Green Pepper Topping for Large Pizza **(0 cal/0 g fat/0 g fiber)**
Mushrooms Topping for Large Pizza **(0 cal/0 g fat/0 g fiber)**
Ripe (Black) Olives Topping for Large Pizza **(10 cal/0.5 g fat/0 g fibers)**
Pineapple Topping for Large Pizza **(15 cal/0 g fat/0 g fiber)**
American Cheese Topping for Large Pizza **(45 cal/4 g fat/0 g fiber)**

Cheddar Cheese Topping for Large Pizza (35 cal/3 g fat/0 g fiber)
Provolone Cheese Topping for Large Pizza (60 cal/4.5 g fat/0 g fiber)
Anchovies Topping for Large Pizza (0 cal/0 g fat/0 g fiber)
Bacon Topping for Large Pizza (60 cal/4 g fat/0 g fiber)
Grilled Chicken Topping for Large Pizza (25 cal/0.5 g fat 0 g fibers) Philly Steak Topping for Large Pizza (15 cal/0.5 g fat/0 g fiber)
Banana Peppers Topping for Large Pizza (0 cal/0 g fat/0 g fibers)
Green Chile Peppers Topping for Large Pizza (0 cal/0 g fat/0 g fiber)
Green Olives Topping for Large Pizza (20 cal/2 g fat/0 g fiber)
Garlic Topping for Large Pizza (15 cal/0 g fat/0 g fiber)
Jalapeno Peppers Topping for Large Pizza (0 cal/0 g fat/0 g fiber)
Tomatoes Topping for Large Pizza (0 cal/0 g fat/0 g fiber)
America's Favorite Topping for Medium Pizza (130 cal/10 g fat/1 g fiber)
Bacon Cheeseburger Topping for Medium Pizza (140 cal/11 g fat/1 g fiber)
Barbecue Feast Topping for Medium Pizza (130 cal/8 g fat/0 g fiber)
Deluxe Feast Topping for Medium Pizza (100 cal/8 g fat/1 g fiber)
ExtravaganZZa Topping for Medium Pizza (160 cal/12 g fat/1 g fiber)
Hawaiian Feast Topping for Medium Pizza (90 cal/6 g fat/1 g fiber)
MeatZZa Feast Topping for Medium Pizza (150 cal/11 g fat/1 g fiber)
Pepperoni Feast Topping for Medium Pizza (130 cal/11 g fat/1 g fiber)
Philly Cheese Steak Topping for Medium Pizza (100 cal/7 g fat/0 g fibe)

Vegi Feast Topping for Medium Pizza **(80 cal/6 g fat/1 g fiber)**
America's Favorite Topping for Large Pizza **(170 cal/14 g fat/1 g fiber)**
Bacon Cheeseburger Topping for Large Pizza **(200 cal/15 g fat/1 g fiber)**
Barbecue Feast Topping for Large Pizza **(170 cal/11 g fat/0 g fiber)**
Deluxe Feast Topping for Large Pizza **(130 cal/10 g fat/1 g fiber)**
ExtravaganZZa Topping for Large Pizza **(200 cal/16 g fat/1 g fiber)**
Hawaiian Feast Topping for Large Pizza **(130 cal/8 g fat/1 g fiber)**
MeatZZa Feast Topping for Large Pizza **(210 cal/17 g fat/1 g fiber)** Pepperoni Feast Topping for Large Pizza **(180 cal/15 g fat/1 g fiber)**
Philly Cheese Steak Topping for Large Pizza **(130 cal/9 g fat/0 g fiber)**
Vegi Feast Topping for Large Pizza **(120 cal/8 g fat/1 g fiber)**
Medium Pizza - 1 slice / 1/8th of pizza
Medium Cheese Hand-Tossed Pizza **(215 cal/8 g fat/1 g fiber)**
Medium Cheese Deep Dish Pizza **(230 cal/12 g fat/3 g fiber)**
Medium Cheese Crunchy Thin Crust Pizza **(215 cal/11 g fat/3 g fiber)**
Medium Extra Cheese Hand-Tossed Pizza **(240 cal/10 g fat/1 g fiber)**
Medium Extra Cheese Deep Dish Pizza **(255 cal/14 g fat/3 g fiber)**
Medium Extra Cheese Crunchy Thin Crust Pizza **(160 cal/11 g fat/1 g fiber)**
Medium Pepperoni Hand-Tossed Pizza **(255 cal/12 g fat/1 g fiber)**
Medium Pepperoni Deep Dish Pizza **(270 cal/16 g fat/3 g fiber)**

Medium Pepperoni Crunchy Thin Crust Pizza **(175 cal/12 g fat/1 g fiber)**
Medium Sausage Hand-Tossed Pizza **(245 cal/11 g fat/1 g fiber)**
Medium Sausage Deep Dish Pizza **(260 cal/15 g fat/3 g fiber)**
Medium Sausage Crunchy Thin Crust Pizza **(165 cal/11 g fat/1 g fiber)**
Medium America's Favorite Hand-Tossed Pizza **(345 cal/18 g fat/2 g fiber)**
Medium America's Favorite Deep Dish Pizza **(360 cal/22 g fat/4 g fiber)**
Medium America's Favorite Crunchy Thin Crust Pizza **(345 cal/21 g fat/4 g fiber)**
Medium Bacon Cheeseburger Hand-Tossed Pizza **(355 cal/19 g fat/2 g fiber)**
Medium Bacon Cheeseburger Deep Dish Pizza **(370 cal/23 g fat/4 g fiber)**
Medium Bacon Cheeseburger Crunchy Thin Crust Pizza **(355 cal/22 g fat/4 g fiber)**
Medium Barbecue Feast Hand-Tossed Pizza **(345 cal/16 g fat/1 g fiber)**
Medium Barbecue Feast Deep Dish Pizza **(360 cal/20 g fat/3 g fiber)**
Medium Barbecue Feast Crunchy Thin Crust Pizza **(345 cal/19 g fat/3 g fiber)**
Medium Deluxe Feast Hand-Tossed Pizza **(315 cal/16 g fat/2 g fiber)**
Medium Deluxe Feast Deep Dish Pizza **(330 cal/20 g fat/4 g fiber)**
Medium Deluxe Feast Crunchy Thin Crust Pizza **(315 cal/19 g fat/4 g fiber)**
Medium ExtravaganZZa Hand-Tossed Pizza **(400 cal/22 g fat/2 g fiber)**
Medium ExtravaganZZa Deep Dish Pizza **(415 cal/26 g fat/4 g fiber)**
Medium ExtravaganZZa Crunchy Thin Crust Pizza **(320 cal/23

g fat/2 g fiber)
Medium Hawaiian Feast Hand-Tossed Pizza **(330 cal/16 g fat/2 g fiber)**
Medium Hawaiian Feast Deep Dish Pizza **(345 cal/20 g fat/4 g fiber)**
Medium Hawaiian Feast Crunchy Thin Crust Pizza **(250 cal/17 g fat/2 g fiber)**
Medium MeatZZa Feast Hand-Tossed Pizza **(390 cal/21 g fat/2 g fiber)**
Medium MeatZZa Feast Deep Dish Pizza **(405 cal/25 g fat/4 g fiber)**
Medium MeatZZa Feast Crunchy Thin Crust Pizza **(310 cal/22 g fat/2 g fiber)**
Medium Pepperoni Feast Hand-Tossed Pizza **(345 cal/19 g fat/2 g fiber)**
Medium Pepperoni Feast Deep Dish Pizza **(360 cal/23 g fat/4 g fiber)**
Medium Pepperoni Feast Crunchy Thin Crust Pizza **(345 cal/22 g fat/4 g fiber)**
Medium Philly Cheese Steak Hand-Tossed Pizza **(315 cal/15 g fat/1 g fiber)**
Medium Philly Cheese Steak Deep Dish Pizza **(330 cal/19 g fat/3 g fiber)**
Medium Philly Cheese Steak Crunchy Thin Crust Pizza **(315 cal/18 g fat/3 g fiber)**
Medium Vegi Feast Hand-Tossed Pizza **(320 cal/16 g fat/2 g fiber)**
Medium Vegi Feast Deep Dish Pizza **(335 cal/20 g fat/4 g fiber)**
Medium Vegi Feast Crunchy Thin Crust Pizza **(240 cal/17 g fat/2 g fiber)**
Large Pizza - 1 slice / 1/8th of pizza
Large Cheese Hand-Tossed Pizza **(290 cal/9 g fat/3 g fiber)**
Large Cheese Deep Dish Pizza **(320 cal/14 g fat/5 g fiber)**
Large Cheese Crunchy Thin Crust Pizza **(180 cal/9.5 g fat/2 g fiber)**
Large Extra Cheese Hand-Tossed Pizza **(320 cal/11.5 g fat/3**

g fiber)
Large Extra Cheese Deep Dish Pizza **(350 cal/16.5 g fat/5 g fiber)** Large Extra Cheese Crunchy Thin Crust Pizza **(210 cal/12 g fat/2 g fiber)**
Large Pepperoni Hand-Tossed Pizza **(340 cal/13.5 g fat/3 g fiber)**
Large Pepperoni Deep Dish Pizza **(370 cal/18.5 g fat/5 g fiber)**
Large Pepperoni Crunchy Thin Crust Pizza **(230 cal/14 g fat/2 g fiber)**
Large Sausage Hand-Tossed Pizza **(350 cal/14.5 g fat/4 g fiber)**
Large Sausage Deep Dish Pizza **(380 cal/19.5 g fat/6 g fiber)**
Large Sausage Crunchy Thin Crust Pizza **(240 cal/15 g fat/3 g fiber)**
Large America's Favorite Hand-Tossed Pizza **(460 cal/23 g fat/4 g fiber)**
Large America's Favorite Deep Dish Pizza **(490 cal/28 g fat/6 g fiber)**
Large America's Favorite Crunchy Thin Crust Pizza **(350 cal/23.5 g fat/3 g fiber)**
Large Bacon Cheeseburger Hand-Tossed Pizza **(490 cal/24 g fat/4 g fiber)**
Large Bacon Cheeseburger Deep Dish Pizza **(520 cal/29 g fat/6 g fiber)**
large Bacon Cheeseburger Crunchy Thin Crust Pizza **(380 cal/24.5 g fat/3 g fiber)**
Large Barbecue Feast Hand-Tossed Pizza **(460 cal/20 g fat/3 g fiber)**
Large Barbecue Feast Deep Dish Pizza **(490 cal/25 g fat/5 g fiber)**
Large Barbecue Feast Crunchy Thin Crust Pizza **(350 cal/20.5 g fat/2 g fiber)**
Large Deluxe Feast Hand-Tossed Pizza **(420 cal/19 g fat/4 g fiber)**
Large Deluxe Feast Deep Dish Pizza **(450 cal/24 g fat/6 g

fiber)
Large Deluxe Feast Crunchy Thin Crust Pizza **(310 cal/19.5 g fat/3 g fiber)**
Large ExtravaganZZa Hand-Tossed Pizza **(520 cal/28 g fat/4 g fiber)**
Large ExtravaganZZa Deep Dish Pizza **(550 cal/33 g fat/6 g fiber)**
Large ExtravaganZZa Crunchy Thin Crust Pizza **(550 cal/33 g fat/6 g fiber)**
Large Hawaiian Feast Hand-Tossed Pizza **(450 cal/20 g fat/4 g fiber)**
Large Hawaiian Feast Deep Dish Pizza **(480 cal/25 g fat/6 g fiber)** Large Hawaiian Feast Crunchy Thin Crust Pizza **(340 cal/20 g fat/3 g fiber)**
Large MeatZZa Feast Hand-Tossed Pizza **(530 cal/29 g fat/4 g fiber)**
Large MeatZZa Feast Deep Dish Pizza **(560 cal/34 g fat/6 g fiber)**
Large MeatZZa Feast Crunchy Thin Crust Pizza **(420 cal/29 g fat/3 g fiber)**
Large Pepperoni Feast Hand-Tossed Pizza **(470 cal/24 g fat/4 g fiber**
Large Pepperoni Feast Deep Dish Pizza **(500 cal/29 g fat/6 g fibers)** Large Pepperoni Feast Crunchy Thin Crust Pizza **(360 cal/24.5 g fat/3 g fiber)**
Large Philly Cheese Steak Hand-Tossed Pizza **(420 cal/18 g fat/3 g fiber)**
Large Philly Cheese Steak Deep Dish Pizza **(450 cal/23 g fat/5 g fiber)**
Large Philly Cheese Steak Crunchy Thin Crust Pizza **(310 cal/18.5 g fat/2 g fiber)**
Large Vegi Feast Hand-Tossed Pizza **(440 cal/20 g fat/4 g fiber)**
Large Vegi Feast Deep Dish Pizza **(470 cal/25 g fat/6 g fiber)**
Large Vegi Feast Crunchy Thin Crust Pizza **(330 cal/20 g fat/3 g fiber)**

Einstein Bros. Bagels

Paninis
Italian Chicken Panini **(690 cal/27 g fat/3 g fiber)**
Country Grilled Cheese Panini **(540 cal/20 g fat/3 g fiber)**
Cheese Stick Panini **(690 cal/29 g fat/2 g fiber)**
Ham & Cheese Panini **(620 cal/22 g fat/2 g fiber)**
Cali Club Panini **(750 cal/34 g fat/3 g fiber)**

Sandwiches
Tasty Turkey Sandwich on Asiago Bagel **(600 cal/18 g fat/3 g fiber)**
Veg Out Sandwich on Sesame Bagel **(500 cal/13 g fat/4 g fiber)**
Club Mex Sandwich on Challah **(730 cal/38 g fat/3 g fiber)**
Einstein Club on Grilled Rustic White **(670 cal/29 g fat/4 g fiber)**
Roasted Turkey Sandwich on Artisan Wheat **(590 cal/28 g fat/5 g fiber)**
Black Forest Ham Sandwich on Challah Roll **(570 cal/23 g fat/3 g fiber)**
Low-fat 100% Albacore Tuna Salad Sandwich on Artisan Wheat **(400 cal/9 g fat/5 g fiber)**
Cobbie Sandwich on Challah **(620 cal/29 g fat/5 g fiber)**
Hummus & Feta Sandwich on Ciabatta **(450 cal/10 g fat/5 g fiber)**

Salads
Bros Bistro Salad **(810 cal/69 g fat/4 g fiber)**
Chicken Chipotle Salad **(630 cal/40 g fat/7 g fiber)**
Asiago Chicken Ceasar Salad **(740 cal/54 g fat/3 g fiber)**

Soups
Broccoli Sharp Cheddar Soup [14 oz] **(380 cal/23 g fat/1 g fiber)**

Soups
Chicken Noodle Soup [1 bowl] **(160 cal/7 g fat/2 g fiber)**
Caribbean Crab Chowder [1 bowl] **(520 cal/38 g fat/4 g fiber)**
Chicken & Wild Rice Soup [1 bowl] **(440 cal/9 g fat/5 g fiber)**
Low-Fat Vegetarian Minestrone Soup [1 bowl] **(360 cal/10 g**

fat/6 g fiber)
New England Clam Chowder [1 bowl] (370 cal/25 g fat/1 g fiber)
Turkey Chili [1 bowl] (330 cal/11 g fat/6 g fiber)
Sweets
Apple Cinnamon Coffee Cake (660 cal/25 g fat/2 g fiber)
Banana Nut Muffin (640 cal/32 g fat/2 g fiber)
Blueberry Coffee Cake (610 cal/25 g fat/2 g fiber)
Blueberry Muffin (540 cal/22 g fat/1 g fiber)
Chocolate Chip Coffee Cake (730 cal/31 g fat/2 g fiber)
Cinnamon Twist (370 cal/21 g fat/1 g fiber)
Cinnamon Walnut Strudel (550 cal/31 g fat/3 g fiber)
Heavenly Chocolate Chip Cookie (389 cal/19 g fat/2 g fiber)
Honey Roasted Peanut Butter (389 cal/20 g fat/2 g fiber)
Lemon Poundcake (510 cal/28 g fat/1 g fiber)
Marble Poundcake (370 cal/20 g fat/1 g fiber)
Oatmeal Raisin Cookie (319 cal/10 g fat/2 g fiber)
Breakfast
Turkey Sausage & Cheddar Frittata Sandwich (660 cal/23 g fat/2 g fiber)
Black Forest Ham & Swiss Frittata Sandwich (660 cal/21 g fat/2 g fiber)
Smoked Bacon & Cheddar Frittata Sandwich (680 cal/26 g fat/2 g fiber)
Cheddar Omelet Sandwich (590 cal/20 g fat/2 g fiber)
Santa Fe Frittata Sandwich (720 cal/28 g fat/2 g fiber)
Steak & Egg Ranchero Sandwich (690 cal/27 g fat/2 g fiber)
Yogurt Parfait (220 cal/1 g fat/4 g fiber)
Spinach & Bacon Panini (930 cal/49 g fat/3 g fiber)
Lox & Bagel (660 cal/27 g fat/3 g fiber)
Bagels
Plain Bagel [1 bagel] (320 cal/1 g fat/2 g fiber)
Wild Blueberry Bagel [1 bagel] (350 cal/1 g fat/3 g fiber)
Cinnamon Raisin Swirl Bagel [1 bagel] (350 cal/1 g fat/2 g fiber)
Cinnamon Sugar Bagel [1 bagel] (510 cal/21 g fat/2 g fiber)
Cranberry Bagel [1 bagel] (350 cal/1 g fat/3 g fiber)

Sesame Dipd Bagel [1 bagel] **(380 cal/5 g fat/3 g fiber)**
Potato Bagel [1 bagel] **(350 cal/4.5 g fat/2 g fiber)**
Poppy Dip Bagel [1 bagel] **(350 cal/2 g fat/2 g fiber)**
Chocolate Chip Bagel [1 bagel] **(370 cal/3 g fat/3 g fiber)**
Asiago Bagel [1 bagel] **(360 cal/3 g fat/2 g fiber)**
Honey Whole Wheat Bagel [1 bagel] **(320 cal/1 g fat/3 g fiber)**
Everything Bagel [1 bagel] **(340 cal/2 g fat/2 g fiber)**
Egg Bagel [1 bagel] **(340 cal/3 g fat/2 g fiber)**
Sun-Dried Tomato Bagel [1 bagel] **(320 cal/1 g fat/3 g fiber)**
Chopped Onion Bagel [1 bagel] **(330 cal/1 g fat/2 g fiber)**
Jalapeno Bagel [1 bagel] **(310 cal/1 g fat/2 g fibers)**
Pumpernickel Bagel [1 bagel] **(320 cal/1 g fat/3 g fiber)**
Dutch Apple [1 bagel] **(390 cal/6 g fat/4 g fiber)**
Salt Bagel [1 bagel] **(330 cal/1 g fat/2 g fiber)**
Powerbagel Bagel [1 bagel] **(410 cal/5 g fat/4 g fiber)**

Shmears

Plain Shmear [2 Tbsp] **(70 cal/7 g fat/0 g fiber)**
Onion & Chive Shmear [2 Tbsp] **(70 cal/6 g fat/0 g fiber)**
Smoked Salmon Shmear [2 Tbsp] **(60 cal/6 g fat/0 g fiber)**
Plain Reduced Fat Shmear [2 Tbsp] **(60 cal/5 g fat/0 g fiber)**
Maple Raisin & Walnut Reduced Fat Shmear [2 Tbsp] **(60 cal/5 g fat/0 g fiber)**
Garden Veggie Reduced Fat Shmear [2 Tbsp] **(60 cal/5 g fat/0 g fiber)**
Honey Almond Reduced Fat Shmear [2 Tbsp] **(70 cal/5 g fat/0 g fiber)**
Strawberry Reduced Fat Shmear [2 Tbsp] **(70 cal/5 g fat/0 g fiber)**
Jalapeno Salsa Reduced Fat Shmear [2 Tbsp] **(60 cal/5 g fat/0 g fiber)**
Sun-Dried Tomato Reduced Fat Shmear [2 Tbsp] **(60 cal/5 g fat/0 g fiber)**
Blueberry Reduced Fat Shmear [2 Tbsp] **(70 cal/5 g fat/0 g fiber)**

Beverages

Cafe Caramel Frozen Drink [18 oz.] **(600 cal/16 g fat/0 g**

fiber)
Cafe Latte Frozen Drink [18 oz.] **(460 cal/18 g fat/0 g fiber)**
Cafe Mocha Frozen Drink [18 oz.] **(570 cal/14 g fat/0 g fiber)**
Strawberry Frozen Drink [18 oz.] **(440 cal/19 g fat/3 g fiber)**
Vanilla Frozen Drink [18 oz.] **(580 cal/31 g fat/0 g fiber)**
Cookies & Cream Frozen Drink [18 oz.] **(690 cal/36 g fat/1 g fiber)**
Cappuccino [Regular made with 2% milk/12oz] **(90 cal/3.5 g fat/0 g fiber)**
Cafe Latte [Regular made with 2% milk/12oz] **(140 cal/5 g fat/0 g fiber)**
Cafe Mocha [Regular made with 2% milk/12oz] **(230 cal/6 g fat/0 g fiber)**
SpontaneiTEA [1 Drink/24 oz] **(50 cal/0 g fat/0 g fiber)**
Mels Cool Cap [Large/16 oz] **(290 cal/16 g fat/0 g fiber)**
Blackberry Lemonade [1 Drink/15oz] **(310 cal/0 g fat/0 g fiber)**

Kentucky Fried Chicken

Salads & More
Roasted Caesar Salad w/o Dressing & Croutons **(220 cal/9 g fat/3 g fiber)**
Crispy Caesar Salad w/o Dressing & Croutons **(370 cal/19 g fat/3 g fiber)**
Caesar Side Salad w/o Dressing & Croutons **(50 cal/3 g fat/1 g fiber)**
Roasted BLT Salad w/o Dressing **(210 cal/7 g fat/4 g fiber)**
Crispy BLT Salad w/o Dressing **(350 cal/17 g fat/4 g fiber)**
House Side Salad w/o Dressing **(15 cal/0 g fat/1 g fiber)**
Hidden Valley Original Ranch Dressing [1 packet] **(200 cal/20 g fat/0 g fiber)**
Hidden Valley Original Ranch Fat Free Dressing [1 packet] **(35 cal/0 g fat/0 g fiber)**
Hidden Valley Golden Italian Light Dressing [1 packet] **(45 cal/2.5 g fat/0 g fiber)**
KFC Creamy Parmesan Caesar Dressing [1 packet] **(260 cal/26 g fat/0 g fiber)**
KFC Parmesan Garlic Croutons Pouch [1 packet] **(70 cal/3 g fat/0 g fiber)**
KFC Famous Bowls: Mashed Potato w/Gravy **(720 cal/32 g fat/5 g fiber)**
KFC Famous Bowls: Rice w/Gravy **(610 cal/25 g fat/4 g fiber/)**

Sandwiches
KFC Snacker **(320 cal/16 g fat/2 g fiber)**
KFC Snacker: Buffalo **(260 cal/8 g fat/2 g fiber)**
KFC Snacker: Fish **(270 cal/10 g fat/2 g fiber)**
KFC Snacker: Ultimate Cheese **(280 cal/11 g fat/1 g fiber)**
Honey BBQ KFC Snacker **(220 cal/3.5 g fat/2 g fiber)**
Honey BBQ Sandwich **(300 cal/6 g fat/1 g fiber)**
Triple Crunch Sandwich **(650 cal/34 g fat/3 g fiber)**
Double Crunch Sandwich **(530 cal/28 g fat/3 g fiber)**
Crispy Twister **(670 cal/38 g fat/3 g fiber)**
Oven Roasted Twister **(510 cal/23 g fat/4 g fiber)**

Tender Roast Sandwich **(390 cal/19 g fat/1 g fiber)**
Tender Roast Sandwich w/o Sauce **(260 cal/5 g fat/1 g fiber)**
Chicken
Original Recipe Chicken: Whole Wing **(150 cal/9 g fat/0 g fiber)**
Original Recipe Chicken: Breast **(380 cal/19 g fat/0 g fiber)**
Original Recipe Chicken: Breast w/o skin **(140 cal/3 g fat/0 g fiber)**
Original Recipe Chicken: Drumstick **(140 cal/8 g fat/0 g fiber)**
Original Recipe Chicken: Thigh **(360 cal/25 g fat/0 g fiber)**
Extra Crispy Chicken: Whole Wing **(190 cal/12 g fat/0 g fiber)**
Extra Crispy Chicken: Breast **(460 cal/28 g fat/0 g fiber)**
Extra Crispy Chicken: Drumstick **(160 cal/10 g fat/0 g fiber)**
Extra Crispy Chicken: Thigh **(370 cal/26 g fat/0 g fiber**
Strips
Crispy Strips: 3 **(400 cal/24 g fat/0 g fiber)**
Crispy Strips: 2 **(270 cal/16 g fat/0 g fiber)**
Popcorn Chicken
Popcorn Chicken: Kids **(270 cal/16 g fat/1 g fiber)**
Popcorn Chicken: Individual **(380 cal/21 g fat/0 g fiber)**
Popcorn Chicken: Large **(560 cal/31 g fat/1 g fiber)**
Popcorn Chicken: Family **(1210 cal/68 g fat/1 g fiber)**
Pot Pie
Chicken Pot Pie **(770 cal/40 g fat/5 g fiber)**
Wings
HBBQ Wings [6] **(540 cal/33 g fat/1 g fiber)**
Boneless HBBQ Wings [6] **(510 cal/24 g fat/1 g fiber)**
Fiery Buffalo Wings [6] **(440 cal/26 g fat/3 g fiber)**
Boneless Fiery Buffalo Wings [6] **(520 cal/25 g fat/1 g fiber)**
Sweet & Spicy Wings [6] **(460 cal/26 g fat/3 g fiber)**
Boneless Sweet & Spicy Wings [6] **(540 cal/24 g fat/1 g fiber)**
Hot Wings [6] **(450 cal/29 g fat/1 g fiber)**

Sides
Biscuit (190 cal/10 g fat/0 g fiber)
Green Beans (50 cal/1.5 g fat/2 g fiber)
Seasoned Rice (150 cal/1 g fat/2 g fiber)
Mashed Potatoes w/o Gravy (110 cal/4 g fat/1 g fiber)
Mashed Potatoes w/Gravy (130 cal/4.5 g fat/1 g fiber)
Macaroni and Cheese (180 cal/8 g fat/0 g fiber)
Potato Wedges (240 cal/12 g fat/3 g fiber)
Corn on the Cob: 3" (70 cal/1.5 g fat/3 g fiber)
Corn on the Cob: 5.5" (150 cal/3 g fat/7 g fiber)
Baked Beans (230 cal/1 g fat/7 g fiber)
Potato Salad (180 cal/9 g fat/1 g fiber)
Cole Slaw (190 cal/11 g fat/3 g fiber)
Baked! Cheetos (120 cal/4.5 g fat/0 g fiber)

Desserts
Quaker Chewy S'mores Granola Bar (110 cal/2 g fat/1 g fiber)
Apple Pie Mini's [3] (400 cal/22 g fat/2 g fiber)
Double Choc. Chip Cake (400 cal/29 g fat/2 g fiber)
Lil' Bucket Fudge Brownie (270 cal/9 g fat/1 g fiber)
Lil' Bucket Lemon Creme (400 cal/14 g fat/2 g fiber)
Lil' Bucket Chocolate Cream (270 cal/13 g fat/2 g fiber)
Lil' Bucket Strawberry Short Cake (200 cal/6 g fat/0 g fiber)
Pecan Pie Slice (480 cal/21 g fat/2 g fiber)
Apple Pie Slice (290 cal/11 g fat/2 g fiber)
Lemon Meringue Pie Slice (240 cal/9 g fat/1 g fiber)
Sweet Potato Pie Slice (340 cal/16 g fat/1 g fiber)

Legal Seafood

From the Grill (plain or cajun,
LDP Shrimp, 7 pieces **(270 cal/14.7 g fat)**
LDP Scallops, 5 oz **(245 cal/13.5 g fat)**
LDP Tuna, 5 oz **(273 cal/13.9 g fat)**
LDP Haddock, 5 oz **(244 cal/13.7 g fat)**
LDP Chicken, 5-6 oz **(268 cal/10.2 g fat)**
Steamed Items
Steamed Lobsters (with a choice of two side sides - info below calculated without
butter
1.25 - 1.50 lb **(142 cal/.5 g fat)**
1.50 - 1.75 lb **(170 cal/.6 g fat)**
2.00 - 2.50 lb **(240 cal/.9 g fat)**
Fisherman's Pack (with sweet potatoes, vegetables & cheese)
with Cod, 10 oz **(441 cal/12 g fat)**
with Shrimp, 12 pieces **(418 cal/13.2 g fat) Bamboo**
Steamed (Asian glazed with steamed vegetables & a choice of one
side -
LDP Shrimp, 5 oz **(352 cal/2.4 g fat)**
LDP Scallops, 5 oz **(297 cal/.8 g fat)**
LDP Haddock, 5 oz **(295 cal/.9 g fat)**
Side Orders (ala carte)
Baked Potato **(220 cal/.1 g fat)**
Steamed Asparagus **(33 cal/.2 g fat)**
Steamed Snap Peas **(94 cal/0 g fat)**
Jasmine White Rice **(242 cal/.3 g fat)**
George's Cole Slaw **(155 cal/10.2 g fat)**
Steamed Broccoli **(40 cal/.3 g fat)**
Appetizers & Salads
Lite Clam Chowder, cup **(80 cal/0 g fat)**
Lite Clam Chowder, bowl **(120 cal/0 g fat)**
Steamed Mussels w/garlic & white wine **(352 cal/5.2 g fat)**
Steamers **(151 cal/.9 g fat)**

Steamers w/1 oz of drawn butter **(367 cal/24 g fat)**
LDP Mixed Green Salad w/Harriet's Low fat raspberry vinaigrette
(75 cal/2.3 g fat)
LDP Mixed Green Salad w/Harriet's Low fat raspberry vinaigrette,
topped with Crabmeat Salad **(293 cal/9.8 g fat)**
LDP Mixed Green Salad w/Harriet's Low fat raspberry vinaigrette,
topped with Lobster Salad **(413 cal/19.7 g fat)**
LDP Seafood Antipasto (no cheese) w/Harriet's Low fat raspberry vinaigrette **(448 cal/10 g fat)**
Steamed Shrimp Wontons **(512 cal/8.9 g fat)**
Blackened Raw Tuna Sashimi **(292 cal/12.4 g fat)**
Jumbo Shrimp Cocktail **(212 cal/1.4 g fat)**
Raw Oysters **(37 cal/.7 g fat)**
Raw Littleneck Clams **(48 cal/.3 g fat)**
Raw Cherrystone Clams **(88 cal/.5 g fat)**
All Raw Bar Items served with:
1.5 fl oz of cocktail sauce **(38 cal/0 g fat)**
1.5 fl oz horseradish **(79 cal/7.2 g fat)**
1.5 fl oz of champagne mignonette **(15 cal/.6 g fat)**
1.5 fl oz of chili lime salsa **(11 cal/.13 g fat)**

Macaroni Grill

Antipasti
Calamari Fritti **(1000 cal/77 g fat/2 g fiber)**
Mozzarella Fritti **(880 cal/63 g fat/3 g fiber)**
Mushroom Ravioli **(820 cal/60 g fat/3 g fiber)**
Mussels Tarantina **(980 cal/68 g fat/2 g fiber)**
Peasant Bread [1 loaf] **(500 cal/12 g fat/4 g fiber)**
Romano's Sampler: All 3 **(1400 cal/97 g fat/5 g fiber)**
Romano's Sampler: Fried Calamari only **(350 cal/23 g fat/1 g fiber)**
Romano's Sampler: Fried Mozzarella only **(480 cal/32 g fat/1 g fiber)**
Romano's Sampler: Tomato Bruschetta only **(450 cal/33 g fat/2 g fiber)**
Romano's Sampler: Garnish only **(60 cal/4 g fat/1 g fiber)**
Shrimp & Artichoke Dip **(1060 cal/52 g fat/9 g fiber)**
Tomato Bruschetta **(830 cal/54 g fat/7 g fiber)**
Pizza & Calzonetto
BBQ Chicken Pizza [1 pizza] **(970 cal/24 g fat/6 g fiber)**
Pizza Margherita [1 pizza] **(1010 cal/34 g fat/7 g fiber)**
Chicken Pesto Pizza [1 pizza] **(1780 cal/94 g fat/12 g fiber)**
Sicilian Pizza [1 pizza] **(1440 cal/69 g fat/7 g fiber)**
Grilled Chicken Caesar Calzonetto [1 calzonetto] **(1540 cal/88 g fat/8 g fiber)**
Grilled Chicken Caesar Calzonetto: Half [1/2 calzonetto] **(770 cal/44 g fat/4 g fiber)**
Salads
Caesar della Casa/House **(260 cal/21 g fat/2 g fiber)**
Caesar della Casa/House w/o dressing **(110 cal/5 g fat/2 g fiber)**
Garden della Casa/House **(240 cal/15 g fat/3 g fiber)**
Garden della Casa/House w/o dressing **(130 cal/5 g fat/3 g fiber)**
Chicken Caesar **(840 cal/64 g fat/6 g fiber)**
Chicken Caesar w/o dressing **(380 cal/15 g fat/6 g fiber)**
Chicken Florentine **(840 cal/53 g fat/7 g fiber)**

Chicken Florentine w/o dressing **(490 cal/19 g fat/7 g fiber)**
Insalata Blu **(650 cal/55 g fat/5 g fiber)**
Insalata Blu w/o dressing **(440 cal/36 g fat/5 g fiber)**
Insalata Blu w/Chicken **(770 cal/57 g fat/5 g fiber)**
Insalata Blu w/Chicken w/o dressing **(570 cal/38 g fat/5 g fiber)**
Insalata Blu w/entree w/dressing: Half [1/2 full] **(380 cal/32 g fat/3 g fiber)**
Mozzarella Alla Caprese: Half Order [3 each] **(260 cal/21 g fat/1 g fiber)**
Mozzarella Alla Caprese: Full Order [5 each] **(460 cal/38 g fat/2 g fiber)**
Steak & Arugula Salad **(990 cal/80 g fat/4 g fiber)**
Steak & Arugula Salad w/o dressing **(670 cal/46 g fat/3 g fiber)**

Soups & Sides
Lentil Bean Soup: Bowl **(360 cal/9 g fat/14 g fiber)**
Lentil Bean Soup: Cup **(180 cal/5 g fat/7 g fiber)**
Minestrone Soup: Bowl **(510 cal/23 g fat/11 g fiber)**
Minestrone Soup: Cup **(380 cal/20 g fat/6 g fiber/39 g carbs)**
Pasta Fagioli Soup: Bowl **(760 cal/31 g fat/21 g fiber)**
Pasta Fagioli Soup: Cup **(450 cal/23 g fat/10 g fiber)**
Pasta Salad **(310 cal/16 g fat/3 g fiber)**
Grilled Asparagus **(30 cal/1 g fat/2 g fiber)**
Sauteed Broccoli **(260 cal/22 g fat/3 g fiber)**

Dressings & Sauces - 1 fl oz
Honey Mustard Dressing **(130 cal/12 g fat/0 g fiber)**
Caesar Dressing Dressing **(160 cal/16 g fat/0 g fiber)**
Creamy Italian Dressing **(110 cal/10 g fat/0 g fiber)**
Wishbone Italian Dressing **(90 cal/8 g fat/0 g fiber)**
Fat-Free Creamy Italian Dressing **(30 cal/0 g fat/1 g fiber)**
Low-Fat Caesar Dressing **(30 cal/2 g fat/0 g fiber)**
Roasted Garlic Lemon Vinaigrette Dressing **(170 cal/17 g fat/0 g fiber)**
Balsamic Vinaigrette Dressing **(100 cal/9 g fat/0 g fiber)**
Toscana Dressing **(160 cal/17 g fat/0 g fiber)**

Basil Aioli Sauce **(130 cal/14 g fat/0 g fiber)**
Pizzaiola Sauce **(30 cal/2 g fat/0 g fiber)**
Amore de La Grill - includes sides
Boursin Filet **(1120 cal/83 g fat/5 g fiber)**
Honey Balsamic Chicken **(1220 cal/67 g fat/10 g fiber)**
Grilled Pork Chops **(1800 cal/107 g fat/8 g fiber)**
Tuscan Ribeye **(1070 cal/76 g fat/5 g fiber)**
Chicken Portobello **(1030 cal/66 g fat/5 g fiber)**
Grilled Salmon Teriyaki **(1290 cal/81 g fat/5 g fiber)**
Simple Salmon: Lunch & Dinner **(580 cal/38 g fat/2 g fiber)**
Pollo Magra "Skinny Chicken" **(310 cal/5 g fat/5 g fiber)**
Grilled Halibut **(840 cal/44 g fat/2 g fiber)**
Clasico Italian
Chicken Marsala: Lunch **(980 cal/59 g fat/4 g fiber)**
Chicken Marsala: Dinner **(1090 cal/66 g fat/4 g fiber)**
Chicken Parmesan: Lunch **(910 cal/37 g fat/4 g fiber)**
Chicken Parmesan: Dinner **(1490 cal/68 g fat/5 g fiber)**
Chicken Scaloppine: Lunch **(1010 cal/64 g fat/6 g fiber)**
Chicken Scaloppine: Dinner **(1110 cal/71 g fat/6 g fiber)**
Eggplant Parmesan: Lunch **(1070 cal/56 g fat/17 g fiber)**
Eggplant Parmesan: Dinner **(1230 cal/64 g fat/23 g fiber)**
Mama's Trio: Lunch & Dinner **(1490 cal/73 g fat/6 g fiber)**
Shrimp Portofino: Lunch **(1090 cal/79 g fat/5 g fiber)**
Shrimp Portofino: Dinner **(1130 cal/80 g fat/5 g fiber)**
Veal Marsala: Lunch & Dinner **(1320 cal/47 g fat/4 g fiber)**
Veal Parmesan: Lunch & Dinner **(1260 cal/63 g fat/6 g fiber)**
Pasta
Carmela's Chicken Rigatoni: Lunch **(1030 cal/65 g fat/5 g fiber)**
Carmela's Chicken Rigatoni: Dinner **(1320 cal/87 g fat/6 g fiber)**
Fettuccine Alfredo: Lunch & Dinner **(1130 cal/81 g fat/4 g fiber)** Fettuccine Alfredo w/Shrimp: Lunch & Dinner **(1330 cal/96 g fat/4 g fiber)**
Fettuccine Alfredo w/Chicken: Lunch & Dinner **(1370 cal/97 g fat/4 g fiber)**
Pasta Milano: Lunch **(890 cal/47 g fat/10 g fiber)**

Pasta Milano: Dinner (1080 cal/55 g fat/13 g fiber)
Penne Rustica: Lunch (1260 cal/70 g fat/6 g fiber)
Penne Rustica: Dinner (1480 cal/78 g fat/8 g fiber)
Sausage & Pepper Classico: Lunch (770 cal/45 g fat/7 g fiber)
Sausage & Pepper Classico: Dinner (860 cal/45 g fat/9 g fiber)
Shrimp Diavolo: Lunch & Dinner (1150 cal/74 g fat/8 g fiber)
Spaghetti & Meatballs w/Tomato Sauce: Lunch (1080 cal/63 g fat/8 g fiber)
Spaghetti & Meatballs w/Tomato Sauce: Dinner (1430 cal/81 g fat/11 g fiber)
Spaghetti & Meatballs w/Meat Sauce: Lunch (1290 cal/79 g fat/8 g fiber)
Spaghetti & Meatballs w/Meat Sauce: Dinner (2270 cal/115 g fat/17 g fiber)

Stuffed Pasta

Lobster Ravioli: Lunch & Dinner (1090 cal/79 g fat/4 g fiber)
Chicken Cannelloni: Lunch (690 cal/37 g fat/3 g fiber)
Chicken Cannelloni: Dinner (1030 cal/55 g fat/4 g fiber)
Traditional Lasagna: Lunch (850 cal/44 g fat/4 g fiber)
Twice Baked Lasagna w/Meatballs: Lunch & Dinner (1360 cal/80 g fat/8 g fiber)

Kids

Chicken Fingerias only (790 cal/61 g fat/1 g fiber)
Kids Fettuccine Alfredo (530 cal/26 g fat/3 g fiber)
Kids Grilled Chicken & Broccoli (380 cal/5 g fat/5 g fiber)
Macaroni 'n Cheese (580 cal/31 g fat/2 g fiber)
Mona Lisa's Cheese Masterpizza (840 cal/20 g fat/6 g fiber)
Mona Lisa's Pepperoni Masterpizza (910 cal/27 g fat/6 g fiber)
Kids Spaghetti & Meatballs w/Tomato Sauce (500 cal/20 g fat/5 g fiber)
Kids Spaghetti & Meatballs w/Meat Sauce (550 cal/24 g fat/5 g fiber)

Kids Sides

Broccoli Crowns [4 oz.] (40 cal/0 g fat/4 g fiber)

Macaroni 'n Cheese: Side [3 oz.] **(350 cal/18 g fat/1 g fiber)**
Shoestring Fries [4 oz.] **(250 cal/15 g fat/2 g fiber)**
Kids Caesar della Casa/House **(170 cal/12 g fat/2 g fiber)**
Kids Garden della Casa/House w/dressing **(150 cal/9 g fat/2 g fiber)**

Desserts

Dessert Ravioli **(1720 cal/89 g fat/3 g fiber)**
Lemon Passion **(1270 cal/69 g fat/0 g fiber)**
New York Cheesecake **(1080 cal/76 g fat/0 g fiber)**
New York Cheesecake w/Caramel Fudge Sauce **(1760 cal/113 g fat/1 g fiber)**
Smothered Chocolate Cake **(1450 cal/90 g fat/6 g fiber)**

Olive Garden

Garden Fare
Capellini Pomodoro: Lunch **(409 cal/9 g fat/6 g fiber)**
Chicken Giardino: Lunch **(408 cal/12 g fat/4 g fiber)**
Shrimp Primavera: Lunch **(483 cal/11 g fat/6 g fiber)**
Linguine alla Marinara: Lunch **(340 cal/6 g fat/5 g fiber)**
Minestrone Soup **(160 cal/1 g fat/6 g fiber)**
Tuscan T-Bone w/Vegetables **(580 cal/32 g fat/0 g fiber)**
Capellini Pomodoro: Dinner **(644 cal/14 g fat/10 g fiber)**
Chicken Giardino: Dinner **(560 cal/15 g fat/7 g fiber)**
Linguine alla Marinara: Dinner **(510 cal/8 g fat/7 g fiber)**
Pork Filettino w/Vegetables: Dinner **(340 cal/9 g fat/0 g fiber)**
Salmon Piccata w/Vegetables: Dinner **(440 cal/21 g fat/0 g fiber)**
Shrimp Primavera: Dinner **(706 cal/18 g fat/8 g fiber)**

Kids Entree
Grilled Chicken Kids Entree **(349 cal/11 g fat/4 g fiber)**

Dressings
Low Fat Italian Dressing [2 fl oz.] **(37 cal/2 g fat/0.5 g fiber)**
Low Fat Parmesan-Peppercorn Dressing [2 fl oz. de] **(45 cal/2 g fat/1 g fiber)**

Appetizers
Breadstick: Plain [1] **(140 cal/1.5 g fat/0 g fiber)**
Bruschetta [1 piece] **(201 cal/19.2 g fat/1.7 g fiber)**
Ciabatta [1/4 loaf] **(240 cal/2 g fat/0 g fiber)**
Sicilian Scampi [4 shrimps] **(458 cal/30.6 g fat/0.8 g fiber)**
Stuffed Mushrooms [6 small mushrooms] **(386 cal/31.4 g fat/1.4 g fiber)**

Entrees
Eggplant Parmigiana: Lunch **(793 cal/39 g fat/8 g fiber)**
Fettuccine Alfredo: Lunch **(850 cal/48 g fat/2 g fiber)**
Lasagna Classico: Lunch [4" x 4.5"] **(858 cal/47.4 g fat/5 g fiber)**
Sausage & Peppers Rustica: Lunch **(884 cal/51 g fat/6 g**

fiber

Chicken Castellina: Dinner **(895 cal/45.5 g fat/3.5 g fiber)**
Chicken Marsala: Dinner **(973 cal/57.4 g fat/9 g fiber)**
Manicotti Formaggio: Dinner [3 pieces] **(798 cal/38 g fat/4 g fiber)**
Mixed Grill: Dinner [w/vegetables & Tuscan potatoes] **(839 cal/43 g fat/5 g fiber)**
Stuffed Chicken Marsala: Dinner [w/Mashed Potatoes] **(1315 cal/86.4 g fat/8 g fiber)**

Panera Bread

Breads
Artisan Country demi: loaf [2 oz] (130 cal/0 g fat/1 g fiber)
Artisan Country miche [2 oz] (120 cal/0 g fat/1 g fiber)
Artisan French baguette [2 oz] (140 cal/0 g fat/1 g fiber)
Artisan French miche [2 oz] (120 cal/0 g fat/1 g fiber)
Artisan Sesame Semolina loaf [2 oz] (130 cal/0.5 g fat/1 g fiber)
Artisan Sesame Semolina miche [2 oz] (120 cal/0.5 g fat/1 g fiber)
Artisan Stone-Milled Rye loaf [2 oz] (120 cal/0 g fat/2 g fiber)
Artisan Stone-Milled Rye miche [2 oz] (120 cal/0 g fat/2 g fiber)
Artisan Three Cheese demi [2 oz] (140 cal/2.5 g fat/2 g fiber)
Artisan Three Cheese loaf [2 oz] (140 cal/2 g fat/1 g fiber)
Artisan Three Cheese miche [2 oz] (130 cal/2 g fat/1 g fiber)
Artisan Three Seed demi [2 oz] (130 cal/0 g fat/1 g fiber)
Asiago Cheese Focaccia [2 oz] (160 cal/6 g fat/1 g fiber)
Basil Pesto Focaccia [2 oz] (160 cal/6 g fat/1 g fiber)
Ciabatta [6 oz] (500 cal/12 g fat/4 g fiber)
Whole Grain baguette [2 oz] (140 cal/1 g fat/3 g fiber)
Whole Grain loaf [2 oz] (150 cal/1 g fat/3 g fiber)
Asiago Cheese demi: loaf [2 oz] (150 cal/4 g fat/1 g fiber)
Cinnamon Raisin loaf [2 oz] (170 cal/3 g fat/1 g fiber)
French baguette [2 oz] (150 cal/1 g fat/1 g fiber)
French loaf: XL loaf [2 oz] (140 cal/1 g fat/1 g fiber)
French roll [2.25 oz] (170 cal/1 g fat/1 g fiber)
Honey Wheat loaf [2 oz] (160 cal/2.5 g fat/2 g fiber)
Rosemary & Onion Focaccia [2 oz] (150 cal/5 g fat/1 g fiber)
Rye loaf [2 oz] (160 cal/3 g fat/2 g fiber)
Sourdough baguette [2 oz] (150 cal/0 g fat/1 g fiber)
Sourdough loaf: XL loaf [2 oz] (130 cal/0 g fat/1 g fiber)
Sourdough roll [2.5 oz] (190 cal/0.5 g fat/2 g fiber)

Sourdough bread bowl [8 oz] **(560 cal/1.5 g fat/5 g fiber)**
Sunflower loaf [2 oz] **(180 cal/6 g fat/2 g fiber)**
Tomato Basil XL loaf [2 oz] **(130 cal/0.5 g fat/1 g fiber)**
White Whole Grain loaf [2 oz] **(140 cal/1.5 g fat/3 g fiber)**
Lower-Carb Italian Herb loaf [1.1 oz slice] **(80 cal/1 g fat/4 g fiber)**
Lower-Carb Pumpkin Seed loaf [1.1 oz slice] **(90 cal/2.5 g fat/4 g fiber)**

Bagels

Asiago Cheese Bagel [4.75 oz] **(350 cal/6 g fat/2 g fiber)**
Blueberry Bagel [4.75 oz] **(330 cal/1 g fat/3 g fiber)**
Chocolate Hazelnut Bagel [4.5 oz] **(400 cal/7 g fat/3 g fiber)**
Cinnamon Crunch Bagel [4.75 oz] **(410 cal/8 g fat/2 g fiber)**
Dutch Apple & Raisin Bagel [4.75 oz] **(370 cal/3 g fat/3 g fiber)**
Everything Bagel [4.25 oz] **(300 cal/1.5 g fat/3 g fiber)**
French Toast Bagel [4.75 oz] **(380 cal/5 g fat/3 g fiber)**
Peanut Butter Banana Crunch Bagel [4.75 oz] **(410 cal/7 g fat/3 g fiber)**
Plain Bagel [4.25 oz] **(290 cal/1 g fat/3 g fiber)**
Sesame Bagel [4.25 oz] **(310 cal/4 g fat/3 g fiber)**
Whole Grain Bagel [4.5 oz] **(340 cal/2.5 g fat/6 g fiber)**

Cream Cheese

Plain Cream Cheese [2 oz] **(200 cal/19 g fat/0 g fiber)**
Reduced-Fat Plain Cream Cheese [2 oz] **(140 cal/13 g fat/0g fiber)**
Reduced-Fat Hazelnut Cream Cheese [2 oz] **(150 cal/12 g fat/1 g fiber)**
Reduced-Fat Honey Walnut Cream Cheese [2 oz] **(160 cal/11 g fat/1 g fiber)**
Reduced-Fat Raspberry Cream Cheese [2 oz] **(150 cal/11 g fat/1 g fiber)**
Reduced-Fat Sun-Dried Tomato Cream Cheese [2 oz] **(140 cal/12 g fat/1 g fiber)**
Reduced-Fat Veggie Cream Cheese [2 oz] **(120 cal/10 g fat/1 g fiber)**

Pastries & Sweets

Cheese Pastry [3.75 oz] **(380 cal/22 g fat/1 g fiber)**
Cherry Pastry [5 oz] **(420 cal/21 g fat/1 g fiber)**
Chocolate Pastry [3.5 oz] **(340 cal/20 g fat/2 g fiber)**
Fresh Apple Pastry [4.5 oz] **(440 cal/24 g fat/2 g fiber)**
Fresh Strawberries & Cream Pastry [4.5 oz] **(350 cal/20 g fat/2 g fiber)**
Caramel Pecan Brownie [4 oz] **(470 cal/24 g fat/2 g fiber)**
Chocolate Raspberry Brownie [3.75 oz] **(370 cal/18 g fat/2 g fiber)**
Very Chocolate Brownie [4 oz] **(460 cal/22 g fat/2 g fiber)**
Chocolate Chipper Cookie [3.25 oz] **(410 cal/20 g fat/2 g fiber)**
Chocolate Duet w/Walnuts Cookie [3.25 oz] **(400 cal/22 g fat/3 g fiber)**
Nutty Chocolate Chipper Cookie [3.25 oz] **(430 cal/24 g fat/3 g fiber)**
Nutty Oatmeal Raisin Cookie [3.25 oz] **(340 cal/14 g fat/3 g fiber)**
Shortbread [2.5 oz] **(350 cal/21 g fat/1 g fiber)**
Carrot Walnut Mini Bundt Cake [4.5 oz] **(430 cal/21 g fat/2 g fiber)**
Lemon Poppyseed Mini Bundt Cake [4.5 oz] **(460 cal/20 g fat/0 g fiber)**
Pineapple Upside-Down Mini Bundt Cake [6 oz] **(520 cal/25 g fat/2 g fiber)**
Cinnamon Chip Scone [4.75 oz] **(530 cal/27 g fat/2 g fiber)**
Golden Raisin Scone [4 oz] **(390 cal/16 g fat/2 g fiber)**
Orange Scone [4.5 oz] **(430 cal/21 g fat/1 g fiber)**
Savory Ham & White Cheddar Scone [4 oz] **(340 cal/17 g fat/1 g fiber)**
Tart Cherry Scone [4 oz] **(380 cal/16 g fat/2 g fiber)**
Wild Blueberry Scone [4.25 oz] **(410 cal/15 g fat/2 g fiber)**
Bear Claw [4.5 oz] **(460 cal/27 g fat/2 g fiber)**
French Croissant [2.25 oz] **(240 cal/14 g fat/1 g fiber)**
Coffee Cake: Cherry-Cheese [2.3 oz] **(210 cal/11 g fat/1 g fiber)**

Muffins & Muffies
Banana Nut Muffie [3 oz] **(230 cal/11 g fat/2 g fiber)**

Banana Nut Muffin [5.75 oz] **(430 cal/19 g fat/4 g fiber)**
Blueberry Muffin [5.75 oz] **(450 cal/17 g fat/4 g fiber)**
Chocolate Chip Muffie [2.5 oz] **(240 cal/10 g fat/2 g fiber)**
Chocolate Chip Muffin [5.75 oz] **(540 cal/22 g fat/5 g fiber)**
Low-Fat Tripleberry Muffin [5 oz] **(270 cal/2.5 g fat/3 g fiber)**
Pumpkin Muffie [3 oz] **(310 cal/7 g fat/1 g fiber)**
Pumpkin Muffin [5.75 oz] **(590 cal/13 g fat/1 g fiber)**

Souffles

Four Cheese Souffle [6 oz] **(470 cal/30 g fat/2 g fiber)**
Spinach & Artichoke Souffle [6.25 oz] **(490 cal/32 g fat/2 g fiber)**
Spinach & Bacon Souffle [6.25 oz] **(530 cal/34 g fat/2 g fiber)**

Sandwiches

Nutrition information provided for salads & sandwiches are for full-size order with all dressings/condiments/toppings.
Nutrition values for You Pick Two salads & sandwiches are approximately one-half of the values provided.
Chicken Bacon Dijon Panini on Artisan Country [13 oz] **(800 cal/27 g fat/4 g fiber)**
Chicken Bacon Dijon Panini on French [10.5 oz] **(680 cal/29 g fat/2 g fiber)**
Frontega Chicken Panini [14 oz] **(870 cal/41 g fat/6 g fiber)**
Portobello & Mozzarella Panini [13 oz] **(750 cal/37 g fat/6 g fiber)**
Smokehouse Turkey Panini on Artisan Three Cheese [12 oz] **(680 cal/23 g fat/4 g fiber)**
Smokehouse Turkey Panini on Asiago Focaccia [13 oz] **(840 cal/37 g fat/5 g fiber)**
Turkey Artichoke Panini [15 oz] **(840 cal/38 g fat/8 g fiber)**
Asiago Roast Beef Sandwich [13 oz] **(670 cal/27 g fat/3 g fiber)**
Bacon Turkey Bravo Sandwich [14 oz] **(740 cal/25 g fat/5 g fiber)**
Chicken Caesar Sandwich on Artisan Three Cheese [14.5 oz] **(750 cal/32 g fat/4 g fiber)**

Chicken Caesar Sandwich on Asiago Focaccia [15.5 oz] **(920 cal/46 g fat/5 g fiber)**
Italian Combo Sandwich [17 oz] **(1100 cal/56 g fat/5 g fiber)**
Mediterranean Veggie Sandwich [14 oz] **(590 cal/13 g fat/10 g fiber)**
Pepperblue Steak Sandwich [14 oz] **(900 cal/42 g fat/6 g fiber)**
Sierra Turkey Sandwich [14 oz] **(960 cal/53 g fat/5 g fiber)**
Turkey Caprese Sandwich [10 oz] **(610 cal/31 g fat/4 g fiber)**
Tuscan Chicken Sandwich [14 oz] **(740 cal/30 g fat/6 g fiber)**
Chicken Salad Sandwich on Artisan Sesame Semolina [13 oz] **(750 cal/27 g fat/5 g fiber)**
Chicken Salad Sandwich on Whole Grain [12.25 oz] **(580 cal/25 g fat/16 g fiber)**
Smoked Ham & Swiss Sandwich on Artisan Stone-Milled Rye [16 oz] **(750 cal/31 g fat/6 g fiber)**
Smoked Ham & Swiss Sandwich on Rye [13 oz] **(680 cal/34 g fat/4 g fiber)**
Smoked Turkey Breast Sandwich on Artisan Country [14 oz] **(590 cal/15 g fat/5 g fiber)**
Smoked Turkey Breast Sandwich on Sourdough [11 oz] **(430 cal/14 g fat/3 g fiber)**
Tuna Salad Sandwich on Honey Wheat [12 oz] **(720 cal/44 g fat/4 g fiber)**
Tuna Salad Sandwich on Whole Grain [14 oz] **(840 cal/44 g fat/10 g fiber)**

Soups
Baked Potato Soup [8 oz] **(230 cal/14 g fat/1 g fiber)**
Boston Clam Chowder Soup [8 oz] **(299 cal/11 g fat/1 g fiber)**
Broccoli Cheddar Soup [8 oz] **(230 cal/16 g fat/1 g fiber)**
Cream of Chicken & Wild Rice Soup [8 oz] **(200 cal/12 g fat/1 g fiber)**
French Onion Soup w/cheese & croutons [8 oz] **(220 cal/10 g fat/2 g fiber)**
French Onion Soup w/o cheese & croutons [8 oz] **(80 cal/3 g**

fat/2 g fiber)
Low-Fat Chicken Noodle Soup [8 oz] **(100 cal/2 g fat/1 g fiber)**
Low-Fat Vegetarian Black Bean Soup [8 oz] **(160 cal/1 g fat/11 g fiber)**
Low-Fat Vegetarian Garden Vegetable Soup [8 oz] **(90 cal/0.5 g fat/2 g fiber)**
Roasted Turkey Noodle Soup [8 oz] **(110 cal/3.5 g fat/1 g fiber)**
Turkey Chickpea Chili [8 oz] **(210 cal/5 g fat/5 g fiber)**
Vegetarian Butternut Squash Soup [8 oz] **(210 cal/9 g fat/1 g fiber)**
Vegetarian Creamy Tomato Soup [8 oz] **(210 cal/15 g fat/3 g fiber)**
Crispani (3 servings per pizza/nutritional values for 1/3rd pizza)
BBQ Chicken Crispani [4 oz or 1/3 pizza] **(380 cal/15 g fat/2 g fiber)**
Pepperoni Crispani [4.25 oz or 1/3 pizza] **(380 cal/18 g fat/2 g fiber)**
Roasted Wild Mushroom Crispani [3.75 oz or 1/3 pizza] **(340 cal/16 g fat/2 g fiber)**
Sweet Sausage & Roasted Peppers Crispani [4.5 oz or 1/3 pizza] **(380 cal/18 g fat/2 g fiber)**
Italian Meat Classic [4.5 oz or 1/3 pizza] **(380 cal/18 g fat/2 g fiber)**
Three Cheese Crispani [3.75 oz or 1/3 pizza] **(340 cal/15 g fat/2 g fiber)**
Tomato & Fresh Basil Crispani [3.75 oz or 1/3 pizza] **(320 cal/13 g fat/2 g fiber)**
Salads
Nutrition information provided for salads & sandwiches are for full-size order with all dressings/condiments/toppings.
Nutrition values for You Pick Two salads & sandwiches are approximately one-half of the values provided.
Asian Sesame Chicken Salad [12 oz] **(430 cal/19 g fat/5 g fiber)**

Bistro Steak Salad [9 oz] **(630 cal/58 g fat/3 g fiber)**
Caesar Salad [10 oz] **(440 cal/32 g fat/4 g fiber)**
Classic Cafe Salad [11 oz] **(400 cal/37 g fat/5 g fiber)**
Fandango Salad [10 oz] **(390 cal/28 g fat/5 g fiber)**
Fresh Fruit Cup: 5 oz **(70 cal/0 g fat/1 g fiber)**
Fresh Fruit Cup: 10 oz **(150 cal/0 g fat/2 g fiber)**
Fuji Apple Chicken Salad [14.5 oz] **(570 cal/30 g fat/5 g fiber)**
Greek Salad [15 oz] **(520 cal/48 g fat/5 g fiber)**
Grilled Chicken Caesar Salad [14 oz] **(560 cal/34 g fat/4 g fiber)**

Dressings

Balsamic Vinaigrette Dressing [2 oz] **(350 cal/36 g fat/0 g fiber/)**
Caesar Dressing [2 oz] **(200 cal/21 g fat/1 g fiber)**
Fat-Free Raspberry Dressing [2 oz] **(50 cal/0.5 g fat/1 g fiber)**
Fuji Apple Vinaigrette Dressing [2 oz] **(210 cal/16 g fat/0 g fiber)**
Greek Dressing [2 oz] **(290 cal/32 g fat/0 g fiber)**
Reduced-Sugar Asian Sesame Vinaigrette Dressing [2 oz] **(110 cal/8 g fat/0 g fiber)**

Beverages

I.C. Cappuccino Chip: Grande [16 oz] **(590 cal/33 g fat/0 g fiber)**
I.C. Cappuccino Chip: Largo [20 oz] **(700 cal/39 g fat/0 g fiber)**
I.C. Caramel: Grande [16 oz] **(550 cal/23 g fat/0 g fiber)**
I.C. Caramel: Largo [20 oz] **(680 cal/27 g fat/0 g fiber)**
I.C. Honeydew Green Tea: Grande [16 oz] **(350 cal/15 g fat/0 g fiber)**
I.C. Honeydew Green Tea: Largo [20 oz] **(390 cal/16 g fat/0 g fiber)**
I.C. Mango: Grande [16 oz] **(350 cal/10 g fat/3 g fiber)**
I.C. Mango: Largo [20 oz] **(390 cal/10 g fat/3 g fiber)**
I.C. Mocha: Grande [16 oz] **(570 cal/25 g fat/2 g fiber)**
I.C. Mocha: Largo [20 oz] **(700 cal/29 g fat/3 g fiber)**

I.C. Mocha Almond: Grande [16 oz] **(540 cal/34 g fat/2 g fiber)**
I.C. Mocha Almond: Largo [20 oz] **(650 cal/40 g fat/2 g fiber)**
I.C. Spice: Grande [16 oz] **(510 cal/22 g fat/0 g fiber)**
I.C. Spice: Largo [20 oz] **(640 cal/25 g fat/1 g fiber)**
Home Style Lemonade: Grande [16 oz] **(90 cal/0 g fat/0 g fiber)**
Home Style Lemonade: Largo [20 oz] **(130 cal/0 g fat/0 g fiber)**
Iced Green Tea: Grande [16 oz] **(100 cal/0 g fat/0 g fiber)**
Iced Green Tea: Largo [20 oz] **(130 cal/0 g fat/0 g fiber)**
Iced Chai Tea Latte [16 oz] **(150 cal/3.5 g fat/0 g fiber)**
Caffe Latte [8.5 oz] **(120 cal/5 g fat/0 g fiber)**
Cappuccino [8.5 oz] **(120 cal/5 g fat/0 g fiber)**
House Latte [10.8 oz] **(310 cal/12 g fat/0 g fiber)**
Caramel Latte [16 oz] **(390 cal/16 g fat/0 g fiber)**
Caffe Mocha [11.5 oz] **(370 cal/15 g fat/2 g fiber)**
Chai Tea Latte [10 oz] **(190 cal/4 g fat/0 g fiber)**
Hot Chocolate [11 oz] **(370 cal/15 g fat/2 g fiber)**

Panera Kids

Deli Ham w/Cheese Sandwich [5.75 oz] **(360 cal/14 g fat/3 g fiber)**
Deli Roast Beef w/Cheese Sandwich [5.75 oz] **(370 cal/13 g fat/3 g fiber)**
Deli Turkey w/Cheese Sandwich [5.75 oz] **(350 cal/12 g fat/3 g fiber)**
Grilled Cheese Sandwich [3.75 oz] **(290 cal/11 g fat/3 g fiber)**
Peanut Butter & Jelly Sandwich [4.5 oz] **(420 cal/16 g fat/5 g fiber)**
Horizon Organic Chocolate Milk [8 oz] **(180 cal/5 g fat/0 g fiber)**
Horizon Organic Milk [8 oz] **(120 cal/4.5 g fat/0 g fiber)**
Horizon Squeezable Yogurt [2 oz] **(70 cal/1 g fat/0 g fiber)**
Organic Apple Juice [8 oz] **(120 cal/0 g fat/0 g fiber)**

Subway

Pizza
Veggie Pizza (8") **(660 cal/20 g fat/5 g fiber)**
Cheese Pizza (8") **(630 cal/19 g fat/4 g fiber)**
Pepperoni Pizza (8") **(730 cal/28 g fat/4 g fiber)**
Toppings for 8" Pizza
Bacon **(70 cal/5 g fat/0 g fiber)**
Green Peppers **(0 cal/0 g fat/0 g fiber)**
Onions **(20 cal/0 g fat/1 g fiber)**
Olives **(15 cal/1 g fat/0 g fiber)**
Pepperoni **(100 cal/1 g fat/0 g fiber)**
Tomatoes **(5 cal/0 g fat/0 g fiber)**
Sausage **(100 cal/9 g fat/0 g fiber)**
6" Subs-Under 6
Includes wheat bread/lettuce/tomatoes/onions/green peppers/pickles/olives
Ham 6" Sub **(290 cal/5 g fat/4 g fiber)**
Oven Roasted Chicken Breast 6" Sub **(330 cal/5 g fat/5 g fiber)**
Roast Beef 6" Sub **(290 cal/5 g fat/4 g fiber)**
Subway Club 6" Sub **(320 cal/6 g fat/4 g fiber)**
Sweet Onion Chicken Teriyaki 6" Sub **(370 cal/5 g fat/4 g fiber)**
Turkey Breast 6" Sub **(280 cal/4.5 g fat/4 g fiber)**
Turkey Breast & Ham 6" Sub **(290 cal/5 g fat/4 g fiber)**
Veggie Delite 6" Sub **(230 cal/3 g fat/4 g fiber)**
6" Subs
Includes wheat bread/lettuce/tomatoes/onions/green peppers/pickles/olives/cheese
Cheese Steak 6" Sub **(360 cal/10 g fat/5 g fiber)**
Chicken & Bacon Ranch 6" Sub **(540 cal/25 g fat/5 g fiber)**
Chicken Parmesan 6" Sub **(500 cal/18 g fat/5 g fiber)**
Chipotle Southwest Cheese Steak 6" Sub **(450 cal/20 g fat/6 g fiber)**
Cold Cut Combo 6" Sub **(410 cal/17 g fat/4 g fiber)**
Italian BMT 6" Sub **(450 cal/21 g fat/4 g fiber)**

Meatball 6" Sub **(560 cal/24 g fat/7 g fiber)**
Spicy Italian 6" Sub **(480 cal/25 g fat/4 g fiber)**
Subway Melt 6" Sub **(380 cal/12 g fat/4 g fiber)**
Tuna 6" Sub **(530 cal/31 g fat/4 g fiber)**
Deli Sandwiches
Includes deli roll/lettuce/tomatoes/onions/green peppers/pickles/olives
Tuna w/Cheese Deli Sandwich **(350 cal/18 g fat/3 g fiber)**
Ham Deli Sandwich **(210 cal/4 g fat/3 g fiber)**
Roast Beef Deli Sandwich **(220 cal/4.5 g fat/3 g fiber)**
Turkey Breast Deli Sandwich **(210 cal/3.5 g fat/3 g fiber)**
Wraps
Chicken & Bacon Ranch Wrap w/cheese **(440 cal/27 g fat/9 g fiber/**
Tuna Wrap w/Cheese **(440 cal/32 g fat/9 g fiber)**
Turkey Breast & Bacon Melt Wrap w/Chipotle Sauce **(380 cal/24 g fat/9 g fiber)**
Turkey Breast Wrap **(190 cal/6 g fat/9 g fiber)**
Salads & Toppings
Grilled Chicken & Baby Spinach Salad [w/o Dressing/croutons] **(140 cal/3 g fat/4 g fiber)**
Subway Club Salad [w/o Dressing/croutons] **(160 cal/4 g fat/4 g fiber)**
Tuna w/Cheese Salad [w/o Dressing/croutons] **(360 cal/29 g fat/4 g fiber)**
Veggie Delite Salad [w/o Dressing/croutons] **(60 cal/1 g fat/4 g fiber)**
Atkins Dressing **(200 cal/22 g fat/0 g fiber)**
Fat Free Italian Dressing **(35 cal/0 g fat/0 g fiber)**
Ranch Dressing [.5 net carb] **(200 cal/22 g fat/0.5 g fiber)**
6" Double Meat
DM Ham 6" Double Meat Sub **(350 cal/7 g fat/4 g fiber/)**
DM Oven Roasted Chicken 6" Double Meat Sub **(400 cal/8 g fat/5 g fiber)**
DM Roast Beef 6" Double Meat Sub **(360 cal/7 g fat/4 g fiber)**
DM Subway Club 6" Double Meat Sub **(420 cal/8 g fat/4 g**

fiber)
DM Sweet Onion Chick. Teriyaki 6" Double Meat Sub **(490 cal/7 g fat/5 g fiber)**
DM Turkey Breast 6" Double Meat Sub **(340 cal/6 g fat/4 g fiber)**
DM Turkey Breast & Ham 6" Double Meat Sub **(360 cal/7 g fat/4 g fiber)**
DM Cold Cut Combo 6" Double Meat Sub **(550 cal/28 g fat/4 g fiber)**
DM Cheese Steak 6" Double Meat Sub **(450 cal/14 g fat/6 g fiber)**
DM Chipotle Southwest Cheese Steak 6" Double Meat Sub **(540 cal/24 g fat/7 g fiber)**
DM Italian BMT 6" Double Meat Sub **(630 cal/35 g fat/4 g fiber)**
DM Meatball 6" Double Meat Sub **(860 cal/42 g fat/10 g fiber)**
DM Turkey Breast/Ham & Bacon Melt 6" Double Meat Sub **(500 cal/17 g fat/4 g fiber)**
6" Promotional & Region
Absolute Angus Steak 6" Sub **(420 cal/20 g fat/4 g fiber)**
Barbecue Rib Patty 6" Sub **(420 cal/19 g fat/4 g fiber)**
Barbecue Chicken 6" Sub **(310 cal/6 g fat/5 g fiber)**
BBQ Steak & Monterey Cheddar Cheese 6" Sub **(390 cal/11 g fat/6 g fiber)**
Big Hot Pastrami/Extreme Toasted Pastrami 6" Sub **(580 cal/30 g fat/4 g fiber)**
Bourbon Chicken 6" Sub **(350 cal/5 g fat/4 g fiber)**
Buffalo Chicken 6" Sub **(390 cal/13 g fat/5 g fiber)**
Chicken Florentine Ciabatta 6" Sub **(510 cal/19 g fat/4 g fiber/)**
Gardenburger 6" Sub **(390 cal/7 g fat/9 g fiber)**
Pastrami 6" Sub **(570 cal/29 g fat/5 g fiber)**
Spicy Pico Chicken 'N Cheese 6" Sub **(360 cal/9 g fat/5 g fiber)**
Subway Seafood Sensation 6" Sub **(450 cal/22 g fat/5 g fiber)**

Sweet Onion Steak Teriyaki 6" Sub **(420 cal/9 g fat/4 g fiber)**
Turkey Breast w/Honey Mustard & Cuc 6" Sub **(310 cal/4.5 g fat/5 g fiber)**
Turkey Pastrami 6" Sub **(330 cal/6 g fat/5 g fiber)**
Tuscan Chicken 6" Sub **(390 cal/8 g fat/5 g fiber)**
Veggi-Max 6" Sub **(390 cal/8 g fat/7 g fiber)**
Breakfast
Cheese Sandwich on Deli Round **(270 cal/9 g fat/3 g fiber)**
Chipotle Steak & Cheese Sandwich on Deli Round **(470 cal/25 g fat/4 g fiber)**
Double Bacon & Cheese Sandwich on Deli Round **(460 cal/24 g fat/3 g fiber)**
Honey Mustard Ham & Egg Sandwich on Deli Round **(270 cal/5 g fat/3 g fiber)**
Western w/Cheese Sandwich on Deli Round **(360 cal/14 g fat/3 g fiber)**
Cheese 6" Sub **(310 cal/9 g fat/3 g fiber)**
Chipotle Steak & Cheese 6" Sub **(510 cal/25 g fat/4 g fiber)**
Double Bacon & Cheese 6" Sub **(500 cal/24 g fat/4 g fiber)**
Honey Mustard Ham & Egg 6" Sub **(310 cal/5 g fat/3 g fiber)**
Western w/Cheese 6" Sub **(400 cal/14 g fat/4 g fiber)**
Cheese Breakfast Wrap **(220 cal/10 g fat/8 g fiber)**
Chipotle Steak & Cheese Breakfast Wrap **(430 cal/27 g fat/9 g fiber)**
Double Bacon & Cheese Breakfast Wrap **(410 cal/25 g fat/8 g fiber)**
Honey Mustard Ham & Egg Breakfast Wrap **(230 cal/7 g fat/8 g fiber)**
Western w/Cheese Breakfast Wrap **(210 cal/16 g fat/8 g fiber)**
Desserts
Chocolate Chip Cookie **(210 cal/10 g fat/1 g fiber)**
Chocolate Chunk Cookie **(220 cal/10 g fat/0 g fiber)**
Double Chocolate Chip Cookie **(210 cal/10 g fat/1 g fiber)**
ookie **(210 cal/10 g fat/0 g fiber)**
Raisin Cookie **(200 cal/8 g fat/1 g fiber)**

Peanut Butter Cookie **(220 cal/12 g fat/1 g fiber)**
Sugar Cookie **(220 cal/12 g fat/0 g fiber)**
White Chip Macadamia Nut Cookie **(220 cal/11 g fat/0 g fiber)**
Apple Pie **(245 cal/10 g fat/1 g fiber)**
Fruit Roll **(50 cal/1 g fat/0 g fiber)**
Misc
Berry Lishus Fruizle Express: small **(110 cal/0 g fat/1 g fiber)**
Berry Lishus w/Banana Fruizle Express: small **(140 cal/0 g fat/2 g fiber)**
Pineapple Delight Fruizle Express: small **(130 cal/0 g fat/1 g fiber)**
Pineapple Delight w/Banana Fruizle Express: small **(160 cal/0 g fat/2 g fiber)**
Peach Pizzazz Fruizle Express: small **(100 cal/0 g fat/0 g fiber)**
Sunrise Refresher Fruizle Express: small **(120 cal/0 g fat/1 g fiber)**
Soups - 10 oz cup
Brown & Wild Rice Soup w/Chicken **(230 cal/11 g fat/1 g fiber)**
Chicken & Dumpling Soup **(140 cal/3.5 g fat/2 g fiber)**
Chili Con Carne **(340 cal/11 g fat/10 g fiber)**
Cream of Broccoli Soup **(140 cal/5 g fat/4 g fiber)**
Cream of Potato Soup w/Bacon **(220 cal/10 g fat/5 g fiber)**
Golden Broccoli Soup **(180 cal/11 g fat/4 g fiber)**
Minestrone Soup **(90 cal/1 g fat/3 g fiber)**
New England Style Clam Chowder **(150 cal/5 g fat/2 g fiber)**
Roasted Chicken Noodle Soup **(90 cal/2 g fat/1 g fiber)**
Tomato Garden Vegetable Soup w/Rotini **(90 cal/0.5 g fat/3 g fiber)**
Vegetable Beef Soup **(100 cal/1.5 g fat/3 g fiber)**
Breads
6" Ciabatta Bread **(220 cal/2 g fat/2 g fiber)**
6" Italian/White Bread **(190 cal/2.5 g fat/1 g fiber)**
6" Wheat Bread **(200 cal/2.5 g fat/3 g fiber)**

6" Parmesan Oregano Bread **(210 cal/3.5 g fat/2 g fiber/)**
6" Honey Oat Bread **(250 cal/3.5 g fat/4 g fiber)**
6" Hearty Italian Bread **(210 cal/2.5 g fat/2 g fiber)**
6" Monterey Cheddar Bread **(240 cal/6 g fat/2 g fiber)**
6" Italian Herbs & Cheese Bread **(240 cal/6 g fat/2 g fiber)**
Deli Style Roll **(170 cal/2.5 g fat/3 g fiber)**
Carb Conscious Wrap **(120 cal/4.5 g fat/8 g fiber)**
Condiments - amount on 6" sub
Bacon [2 strips] **(45 cal/3.5 g fat/0 g fiber)**
Chipotle Southwest Sauce [amount on 6" sub] **(96 cal/10 g fat/0 g fiber)**
Honey Mustard Sauce: Fat Free [amount on 6" sub] **(30 cal/0 g fat/0 g fiber)**
Light Mayonnaise [1 Tbsp] **(50 cal/5 g fat/0 g fiber)**
Mayonnaise [1 Tbsp] **(110 cal/12 g fat/0 g fiber)**
Mustard yellow or deli [amount on 6" sub] **(5 cal/0 g fat/0 g fiber)**
Olive Oil [amount on 6" sub] **(45 cal/5 g fat/0 g fiber)**
Ranch Dressing [amount on 6" sub] **(70 cal/8 g fat/0 g fiber)**
Red Wine Vinaigrette: Fat Free [amount on 6" sub] **(29 cal/0 g fat/0 g fiber)**
Sweet Onion Sauce: Fat Free [amount on 6" sub] **(40 cal/0 g fat/0 g fiber)**
Vinegar [1 tsp] **(0 cal/0 g fat/0 g fiber)**
Banana Peppers [3 rings] **(0 cal/0 g fat/0 g fiber)**
Cucumbers [3 slices] **(5 cal/0 g fat/0 g fiber)**
Green Peppers [3 strips] **(0 cal/0 g fat/0 g fiber)**
Jalapeno Peppers [3 rings] **(5 cal/0 g fat/0 g fiber)**
Lettuce [amount on 6" sub] **(5 cal/0 g fat/0 g fiber)**
Onions [amount on 6" sub] **(5 cal/0 g fat/0 g fiber)**
Pickles [3 chips] **(0 cal/0 g fat/0 g fiber)**
 ves [3 rings] **(5 cal/0 g fat/0 g fiber)**
   3 wheels] **(5 cal/0 g fat/0 g fiber)**
  Amount on 6" sub
  d **(40 cal/3.5 g fat/0 g fiber)**
  r: Shredded **(50 cal/4.5 g fat/0 g fiber)**
  (60 cal/5 g fat/0 g fiber)

Pepperjack **(50 cal/4 g fat/0 g fiber)**
Provolone **(50 cal/4 g fat/0 g fiber)**
Swiss **(50 cal/4.5 g fat/0 g fiber)**
Chicken Patty: Breaded Meat Only **(180 cal/9 g fat/0 g fiber)**
Chicken Patty: Roasted Meat Only **(90 cal/2.5 g fat/0 g fiber)**
Chicken Strips Meat **(80 cal/1.5 g fat/0 g fiber)**
Cold Cut Combo Meats **(140 cal/11 g fat/0 g fiber)**
Ham Meat **(60 cal/2 g fat/0 g fiber)**
Italian BMT Meats **(180 cal/14 g fat/0 g fiber)**
Meatballs Meat **(300 cal/18 g fat/3 g fiber)**
Roast Beef Meat **(70 cal/2 g fat/0 g fiber)**
Seafood Sensation Meat **(190 cal/16 g fat/0 g fiber)**
Steak w/o Cheese Meat **(90 cal/3.5 g fat/1 g fiber)**
Subway Club Meats **(100 cal/3 g fat/0 g fiber)**
Tuna Meat **(260 cal/24 g fat/0 g fiber)**
Turkey Breast Meat **(50 cal/1 g fat/0 g fiber)**
Veggy Patty Meat **(160 cal/5 g fat/3 g fiber)**

Wendy's

Salads & Dressings
Crispy Noodles for Mandarin Chicken Salad [1 pkt] **(60 cal/2 g fat/0 g fiber)**
Roasted Almonds for Mandarin Chicken Salad [1 pkt] **(130 cal/11 g fat/2 g fiber)**
Oriental Sesame Dressing for Mandarin Chicken Salad [1 pkt] **(190 cal/11 g fat/0 g fiber)**
Caesar Chicken Salad [Romaine/Grape Tomatoes/Parmesan Cheese/Diced Chicken] **(180 cal/5 g fat/4 g fiber)**
Homestyle Garlic Croutons for Caesar Chicken Salad [1 pkt] **(70 cal/2.5 g fat/0 g fiber)**
Caesar Dressing for Caesar Chicken Salad [1 pkt] **(120 cal/13 g fat/0 g fiber)**
Chicken BLT Salad [Iceberg/Romaine/Spring Mix/Cucumbers/Grape Tomatoes/Cheddar Cheese/Bacon Pieces/Diced Chicken] **(340 cal/18 g fat/4 g fiber)**
Homestyle Garlic Croutons [1 pkt] **(70 cal/2.5 g fat/0 g fiber)**
Honey Mustard Dressing [1 pkt] **(280 cal/26 g fat/0 g fiber)**
Southwest Taco Salad [Iceberg/Romaine/Diced Tomatoes/Cheddar Cheese/Wendy's Chili] **(440 cal/22 g fat/9 g fiber)**
Reduced Fat Sour Cream for Southwest Taco Salad [1 pkt] **(45 cal/3.5 g fat/0 g fiber)**
Seasoned Tortilla Strips for Southwest Taco Salad [1 pkt] **(110 cal/5 g fat/1 g fiber)**
Ancho Chipotle Ranch Dressing for Southwest Taco Salad [1 pkt] **(110 cal/10 g fat/0 g fiber/4 g carbs)**

Other Dressings
Fat Free French [1 pkt] **(80 cal/0 g fat/0 g fiber)**
Reduced Fat Creamy Ranch [1 pkt] **(100 cal/8 g fat/1 g fiber)**
Low Fat Honey Mustard [1 pkt] **(110 cal/3 g fat/0 g fiber)**
Italian Vinaigrette [1 pkt] **(140 cal/12 g fat/0 g fiber)**
Creamy Ranch [1 pkt] **(230 cal/23 g fat/0 g fiber)**

Blue Cheese [1 pkt] **(260 cal/27 g fat/0 g fiber)**
Thousand Island [1 pkt] **(260 cal/25 g fat/0 g fiber)**
Beverages
Milk: 2% Reduced Fat Milk **(120 cal/4.5 g fat/0 g fiber)**
Milk: 1% Low Fat Chocolate **(170 cal/2.5 g fat/0 g fiber)**
Diet Coke: Medium Cup **(0 cal/0 g fat/0 g fiber)**
Sprite: Medium Cup **(130 cal/0 g fat/0 g fiber)**
Coca-Cola: Medium Cup **(140 cal/0 g fat/0 g fiber)**
Dasani Water **(0 cal/0 g fat/0 g fiber)**
Note about Beverages - [To determine nutritional information for a Kid's size (12 oz.) soft drink-multiply by 0.6; Small (16 oz.) soft drink-multiply by 0.8; Biggie (32 oz.) soft drink-multiply by 1.6.]
Frosty
Junior Original Chocolate Frosty **(160 cal/4 g fat/0 g fiber)**
Small Original Chocolate Frosty **(330 cal/8 g fat/0 g fiber)**
Medium Original Chocolate Frosty **(430 cal/11 g fat/0 g fiber)**
Junior Vanilla Frosty **(150 cal/4 g fat/0 g fiber)**
Small Vanilla Frosty **(310 cal/8 g fat/0 g fiber)**
Medium Vanilla Frosty **(410 cal/10 g fat/0 g fiber)**
Fix 'N Mix Original Chocolate Frosty **(170 cal/4 g fat/0 g fiber)**
Fix 'N Mix Vanilla Frosty **(160 cal/4 g fat/0 g fiber)**
Oreo Cookie Crumbles [1 pkt] **(100 cal/4 g fat/1 g fiber)**
Butterfinger Candy Crumbles [1 pkt] **(130 cal/5 g fat/1 g fiber)**
M&M's Candy Crumbles [1 pkt] **(140 cal/6 g fat/1 g fiber)**
Sides
Side Salad [Iceberg/Romaine/Cucumbers/Grape Tomatoes/Carrots] **(35 cal/0 g fat/2 g fiber)**
Caesar Side Salad [Romaine/Parmesan Cheese/Bacon Pieces] **(70 cal/4.5 g fat/2 g fiber)**
Homestyle Garlic Croutons for Caesar Side Salad [1 pkt] **(70 cal/2.5 g fat/0 g fiber)**
Caesar Dressing for Caesar Side Salad [1 pkt] **(120 cal/13 g fat/0 g fiber)**

Mandarin Orange Cup for Caesar Side Salad [5 oz] **(80 cal/0 g fat/1 g fiber)**
Low Fat Strawberry Flavored Yogurt **(140 cal/1.5 g fat/0 g fiber)**
Granola Topping [1 pkt] **(110 cal/4.5 g fat/1 g fiber)**
Plain Baked Potato [10 oz] **(270 cal/0 g fat/7 g fiber)**
Sour Cream & Chives Baked Potato [Potato w/Reduced Fat Sour Cream & Chives] **(320 cal/4 g fat/7 g fiber)**
Buttery Best Spread [1 pkt] **(50 cal/6 g fat/0 g fiber)**
Small Chili [8 oz] **(220 cal/6 g fat/5 g fiber)**
Large Chili [12 oz] **(330 cal/9 g fat/8 g fiber)**
Hot Chili Seasoning [1 pkt] **(5 cal/0 g fat/0 g fiber)**
Saltine Crackers [2 ea] **(25 cal/0.5 g fat/0 g fiber)**
Cheddar Cheese: shredded [2 tbsp] **(70 cal/6 g fat/0 g fiber)**
Baked Lay's [1 bag] **(130 cal/2 g fat/2 g fiber)**
Kids' Meal French Fries [3.2 oz] **(280 cal/14 g fat/3 g fiber)**
Medium French Fries [5.0 oz] **(440 cal/21 g fat/5 g fiber)**
Biggie French Fries [5.6 oz] **(490 cal/24 g fat/6 g fiber)**
Great Biggie French Fries [6.7 oz] **(590 cal/28 g fat/7 g fiber)**

Chicken Strips

Homestyle Chicken Strips [3 ea] **(410 cal/18 g fat/0 g fiber)**
Deli Honey Mustard Dipping Sauce [1 pkt] **(170 cal/16 g fat/0 g fiber)**
Spicy Southwest Chipotle Dipping Sauce [1 pkt] **(150 cal/15 g fat/0 g fiber)**
Heartland Ranch Dipping Sauce [1 pkt] **(200 cal/22 g fat/0 g fiber)**
Sweet & Spicy Hawaiian Dipping Sauce [1 pkt] **(70 cal/0 g fat/0 g fiber)**
Wild Buffalo Ranch Dipping Sauce [1 pkt] **(180 cal/19 g fat/0 g fiber)**

Chicken Nuggets

4 Piece Kids' Meal Nuggets [4 pc] **(180 cal/11 g fat/0 g fiber)**
5 Piece Nuggets [5 pc] **(220 cal/14 g fat/0 g fiber)**
10 Piece Nuggets [10 pc] **(440 cal/29 g fat/0 g fiber)**

Barbecue Nugget Sauce [1 pkt] **(45 cal/0 g fat/0 g fiber)**
Sweet & Sour Nugget Sauce [1 pkt] **(50 cal/0 g fat/0 g fiber)**
Honey Mustard Nugget Sauce [1 pkt] **(130 cal/12 g fat/0 g fiber)**

Sandwiches

Jr. Hamburger [2 oz. Patty/Ketchup/Mustard/Dill Pickles/Onion/Sandwich Bun] **(280 cal/9 g fat/1 g fiber)**
Jr. Cheeseburger [2 oz. Patty/American Cheese Jr./Ketchup/Mustard/Dill Pickles/Onion/Sandwich Bun] **(320 cal/13 g fat/1 g fiber)**
Jr. Cheeseburger Deluxe [2 oz. Patty/American Cheese/Mayonnaise/Ketchup/Mustard/Dill Pickles/Onion/Tomato/Lettuce/Sandwich Bun] **(360 cal/16 g fat/2 g fiber)**
Jr. Cheeseburger Deluxe w/o mayo [2 oz. Patty/American Cheese Jr./Ketchup/Mustard/Dill Pickles/Onion/Tomato/Lettuce/Sandwich Bun] **(330 cal/13 g fat/2 g fiber)**
Jr. BBQ Cheeseburger [2 oz. Patty/American Cheese Jr./BBQ Sauce/Pickles/Onions/Sandwich Bun] **(330 cal/13 g fat/1 g fiber)**
Jr. Bacon Cheeseburger [2 oz. Patty/American Cheese Jr./Bacon/Mayonnaise/Tomato/Lettuce/Sandwich Bun] **(370 cal/17 g fat/2 g fiber)**
Jr. Bacon Cheeseburger w/o mayo [2 oz. Patty/American Cheese Jr./Bacon/Tomato/Lettuce/Sandwich Bun] **(330 cal/14 g fat/2 g fiber)**
Hamburger: Kids' Meal [2 oz. Patty/Ketchup/Mustard/Dill Pickles/Sandwich Bun] **(270 cal/9 g fat/1 g fiber/33 g carbs)**
Cheeseburger: Kids' Meal [2 oz. Patty/American Cheese Jr./Ketchup/Mustard/Dill Pickles/Sandwich Bun] **(320 cal/13 g fat/1 g fiber)**
Ham & Cheese Sandwich: Kids' Meal [Black Forest Ham/Lettuce/Sandwich Bun] **(240 cal/6 g fat/1 g fiber)**
Turkey & Cheese Sandwich: Kids' Meal [Roasted Turkey

Breast/Lettuce/Sandwich Bun] **(250 cal/6 g fat/1 g fiber)**
Classic Single w/Everything [1/4 lb. Patty/Mayonnaise/Ketchup/Mustard/Dill Pickles/Onion/Tomato/Lettuce/Sandwich Bun] **(420 cal/19 g fat/2 g fiber)**
Classic Single: Plain [1/4 lb. Patty/Sandwich Bun] **(370 cal/16 g fat/1 g fiber)**
Big Bacon Classic [1/4 lb. Patty/American Cheese/Bacon/Mayonnaise/Ketchup/Dill Pickles/Onion/Tomato/Lettuce/Kaiser Roll] **(580 cal/29 g fat/3 g fiber)**
Big Bacon Classic w/o mayo [1/4 lb. Patty/American Cheese/Bacon/Ketchup/Dill Pickles/Onion/Tomato/Lettuce/Kaiser Roll] **(530 cal/25 g fat/3 g fiber)**
Ultimate Chicken Grill Sandwich [Ultimate Chicken Grill Fillet/Honey Mustard Sauce/Tomato/Lettuce/Kaiser Roll] **(360 cal/7 g fat/2 g fiber)**
Spicy Chicken Fillet Sandwich [Spicy Chicken Fillet/Mayonnaise/Tomato/Lettuce/Kaiser Roll] **(510 cal/19 g fat/2 g fiber)**
Spicy Chicken Fillet Sandwich w/o mayo [Spicy Chicken Fillet/Tomato/Lettuce/Kaiser Roll] **(470 cal/15 g fat/2 g fiber)**
Homestyle Chicken Fillet Sandwich [Chicken Fillet/Mayonnaise/Tomato/Lettuce/Kaiser Roll] **(540 cal/22 g fat/2 g fiber)**
Homestyle Chicken Fillet Sandwich w/o mayo [Chicken Fillet/Tomato/Lettuce/Kaiser Roll] **(470 cal/15 g fat/2 g fiber)**
Crispy Chicken Sandwich [Crispy Chicken Patty/Lettuce/Mayonnaise/Sandwich Bun] **(380 cal/15 g fat/1 g fiber)**
Crispy Chicken Sandwich w/o mayo [Crispy Chicken Patty/Lettuce/Sandwich Bun] **(350 cal/12 g fat/1 g fiber)**
Black Forest Ham & Swiss Frescata [Black Forest Ham/Swiss Cheese/Honey Mustard Sauce/Romaine

Lettuce/Tomato/Artisan Bread] **(480 cal/20 g fat/4 g fiber)**
Roasted Turkey & Swiss Frescata [Roasted Turkey Breast/Swiss Cheese/Mayonnaise/Romaine Lettuce/Tomato/Artisan Bread] **(490 cal/21 g fat/4 g fiber)**
Roasted Turkey & Swiss Frescata w/o mayo [Roasted Turkey Breast/Swiss Cheese/Romaine Lettuce/Tomato/Artisan Bread] **(420 cal/15 g fat/4 g fiber)**
Roasted Turkey & Swiss Frescata w/o Cheese [Roasted Turkey Breast/Mayonnaise/Romaine Lettuce/Tomato/Artisan Bread] **(410 cal/14 g fat/4 g fiber)**
Roasted Turkey Frescata w/o mayo/cheese [Roasted Turkey Breast/Romaine Lettuce/Tomato/Artisan Bread] **(350 cal/8 g fat/4 g fiber)**
Frescata Club [Roasted Turkey Breast/Black Forest Ham/Bacon/Mayonnaise/Romaine Lettuce/Tomato/Artisan Bread] **(440 cal/16 g fat/4 g fiber)**
Frescata Club w/o mayo [Roasted Turkey Breast/Black Forest Ham/Bacon/Romaine Lettuce/Tomato/Artisan Bread] **(380 cal/10 g fat/4 g fiber)**
Roasted Turkey & Basil Pesto Frescata [Roasted Turkey Breast/Roasted Red Peppers/Basil Pesto Spread/Romaine Lettuce/Artisan Bread] **(420 cal/16 g fat/4 g fiber)**
Roasted Turkey & Basil Pesto Frescata w/o spread [Roasted Turkey Breast/Roasted Red Peppers/Romaine Lettuce/Artisan Bread] **(350 cal/8 g fat/3 g fiber)**
Frescata Italiana [Genoa Salami/Black Forest Ham/Swiss Cheese/Roasted Red Peppers/Sundried Tomato Vinaigrette/Romaine Lettuce/Artisan Bread] **(510 cal/24 g fat/4 g fiber)**
Frescata Italiana w/o Vinaigrette [Genoa Salami/Black Forest Ham/Swiss Cheese/Roasted Red Peppers/Romaine Lettuce/Artisan Bread] **(470 cal/22 g fat/3 g fiber)**
Frescata Italiana w/o Cheese [Genoa Salami/Black Forest Ham/Roasted Red Peppers/Sundried Tomato Vinaigrette/Romaine Lettuce/Artisan Bread] **(440 cal/18 g fat/4 g fiber)**
Frescata Italiana w/o Cheese/Vinaigrette [Genoa Salami/Black

Forest Ham/Roasted Red Peppers/Romaine Lettuce/Artisan Bread] **(390 cal/15 g fat/3 g fiber)**
Components
2 oz. Hamburger Patty [2 oz precooked] **(100 cal/7 g fat/0 g fiber)**
1/4 lb. Hamburger Patty [1/4 lb precooked] **(210 cal/14 g fat/0 g fiber)**
Ultimate Chicken Grill Fillet [1 pc] **(120 cal/2.5 g fat/0 g fiber)**
Spicy Chicken Fillet [1 pc] **(260 cal/12 g fat/0 g fiber)**
Homestyle Chicken Fillet [1 pc] **(260 cal/12 g fat/0 g fiber)**
Crispy Chicken Patty [1 pc] **(190 cal/11 g fat/0 g fiber)**
Roasted Turkey Breast [4 slices] **(80 cal/1.5 g fat/0 g fiber)**
Genoa Salami [3 slices] **(100 cal/8 g fat/0 g fiber)**
Black Forest Ham [4 slices] **(70 cal/1.5 g fat/0 g fiber)**
Sandwich Bun [1] **(160 cal/2 g fat/1 g fiber)**
Kaiser Roll [1] **(200 cal/2.5 g fat/2 g fiber)**
Artisan Bread [1] **(250 cal/6 g fat/3 g fiber)**
American Cheese Jr. [1 slice] **(45 cal/3.5 g fat/0 g fiber)**
American Cheese [1 slice] **(70 cal/5 g fat/0 g fiber)**
Swiss Cheese [1 slice] **(70 cal/6 g fat/0 g fiber)**
Bacon [1 strip] **(20 cal/1.5 g fat/0 g fiber)**
Mayonnaise [1 tsp] **(30 cal/3 g fat/0 g fiber)**
Honey Mustard Sauce [1 tsp] **(40 cal/3.5 g fat/0 g fiber)**
BBQ Sauce [1 tsp] **(15 cal/0 g fat/0 g fiber)**
Basil Pesto Spread [2 tsp] **(80 cal/8 g fat/0 g fiber)**
Sundried Tomato Vinaigrette [1 tbsp] **(45 cal/3.5 g fat/0 g fiber)**
Dill Pickles [4 ea] **(0 cal/0 g fat/0 g fiber)**
Ketchup [1 tsp] **(5 cal/0 g fat/0 g fiber)**
Mustard [1/2 tsp] **(5 cal/0 g fat/0 g fiber)**
Honey Mustard Sauce [1 tsp] **(0 cal/0 g fat/0 g fiber)**
Iceburg Lettuce [1 leaf] **(0 cal/0 g fat/0 g fiber)**
Romaine Lettuce [1 leaf] **(0 cal/0 g fat/0 g fiber)**
Tomato [1 slice] **(5 cal/0 g fat/0 g fiber)**
Onion [4 rings] **(5 cal/0 g fat/0 g fiber)**
Roasted Red Peppers [2 tbsp] **(10 cal/0 g fat/0 g fiber)**

Week TWELVE

Social Hour and parties

Downing too many cocktails is a fast way to pack on a few pounds. But, if you want to have a drink or two on special occasions, there are definitely drinks that are fairly good choices, and ones you should be avoiding at all costs. For starters, a light beer or a glass of wine each has about 100 calories. But that's not necessarily better than a mixed drink -- *if* you know what to mix your drinks with. A shot of vodka or rum (or most other alcohols) has about 75-100 calories. So if you mix your liquor with something calorie-free, you can keep your cocktail calorie count to about 100, which isn't bad at all. Just don't trick yourself into thinking juices are great mixers. They aren't. They'll likely add 50-75 calories to whatever you're sipping. Calorie-free sodas like Diet Coke, Diet 7Up or diet orange are great mixers. Also, calorie-free soft drinks, like sugar free lemonade or Crystal Light are awesome to use in mixed drinks

On the other hand, the things you want to avoid at all costs are frozen drinks like daquiris, piña coladas, and margaritas. And, of course, you'll want to steer clear of any of those sweet drinks mixed with cream or milk. Good luck, and remember, if you're drinking anything at all, make sure someone else is driving!

My big tip of parties and cocktail hour is the party stance. I stand with a napkin with appetizer on one hand and my wine glass in the other. There is NO way that I can get the food to my mouth, in a lady like fashion, with the glass in my hand. So it appears I always have something to eat, but no way to get it to my mouth. (Which no one ever seems to notice) Therefore, no calories are taken in and no one realized that I am not participating in the foods. I also, set a drink limit and after the first I have the beautiful glass filled with water and a splash of cranberry juice or lemon. I am just as happy as if it were a 300 calorie choice.

Week THIRTEEN

Munching for other than Hunger or taste.

We eat for many reason, habit, boredom, urges, cravings, stressed, being tired. It is important to identify those triggers that you feed with food. If you can determine the reason you are more likely to be able to control it. If you can't identify the trigger, realize food may not be the solution, Exercise and action are a Quick fix. Do something. Anything to get away from the foods you are mindlessly eating.

Tip

Ask yourself what's wrong, and why you're using food to feel better. Talk to friends and family. You feel like you have so many things to do that you're avoiding all of them. Whatever's the culprit, first understand your motivation, then come up with a plan.

Try this:

First, analyze your pattern.

When does boredom eating become a problem for you? Mid-week? Evening? If you know when it's most likely to strike, you'll be better prepared for the battle.

Then come up with alternatives.

Plan what you'll do instead of eating the next time you're bored or stressed. On a post t note, make a list of alternate activities, Have the list with you at all times so you can take it out when you need it.

Make sure your list is full of fulfilling things you *like* to do. Include a variety of things that will suit different moods and times of day. Be sure to add a few items that will help you toward your weight goal, too. Here are some ideas to get you started:

If you have 10 minutes...

- Write down the foods you've eaten so far today.
- Make a grocery list of healthy foods.
- Schedule your next exercise session.
- Write an email to a friend you haven't caught up with in awhile.
- Shop online for a new fitness gadget.

If you have 30 minutes...

- Go for a walk.
- Look through past weeks in your journal. Check out weeks that worked, and see if there's anything you did then that you can do again this week.
- Take a shower.
- Read a favorite book or relax with a magazine.

If you have an hour or more...

- Look through healthy recipe ideas.
- Clean out your closets. Throw away clothes that are now too big, or donate them to charity.
- Go for a long bike ride.
- Start a new project. Whether it's fixing something in your house, building a bookshelf

or starting a garden.
- Take your kids to the park.
- Spend the afternoon at your local museum. This will get you out of the house and walking around, and what better way to get your mind off food than to absorb a little culture?

Avoid mindless consumption of calories that will cause lots of guilt later. It is a terrible cycle to get into, so just don't allow yourself to participate. After all, our health and our future belong singularly to us! If you do fall into the mindless munching, realize that you can only do so much damage in one day. Forgive yourself and begin the next morning on plan …. Journaling your food choices, getting your water and thinking about your healthy choices to include dairy, fruits and vegetables and a good protein source.

Week FOURTEEN

Goals

Goals, do you understand the importance of goals. I did not fully get the impact a goal has on success until I was well into my weight loss journey. Without goals do you every really know when you get there. When to celebrate? I think goals are very important in the weight loss process.

It also helps to keep a goal measurable. Short term and long term. If the journey appears to be too far out of reach, shorten it to mini goals. When it seems like the end is not in reach, I found it very helpful to look at daily goals and success. A day that included at least 5 fruit and vegetable choices and 2 dairy products. Drinking six, eight ounces glasses of water, getting a good protein source and whole grains. By making these changes, I felt very successful. If I was able to work in 30 minutes of walking or other added activity, I felt like a superstar. If I was able to duplicate these successes repeatedly then, I soon saw some very significant weight loss numbers. Repeat this a couple months and I was shopping for a smaller size clothing. Making these goals and reaching them more days than not soon accumulated to over 100 pound loss. Helping others to also reach for these daily goals has yielded repeated success in their health and appearance.

Remember that it is also important to have non food rewards built in. I personally had 10 beautiful roses added to my garden. Each one was the result of another 10 pound loss. Find something that will bring you pleasure and celebrated your mini goals.

Week FIFTEEN

Vacations and Holidays

Vacations pose another set of obstacles in the weight loss and maintenance journey. Many of us have a yearly vacation and some have several a year. One thing I always remember is that vacations are not a once in a lifetime event. And because I will have another to look forward to I do not need to eat every fun and new food that is introduced and offered to me. I love to work with the 90 percent rule. That rule is one to consider, because it has built in fun events with food. For nine meals I follow plan, being conscious of the moment to moment meals and snacks in my mouth and hands, and my plate belongs to my genuine health needs and goals. Family members and friends would look at my choices and recognize that they are suitable to a healthy weight loss journey. Then for the tenth meal, I loosen the rules and have what ever I chose for that meal only. Then for the following meal I match up my choices with that of the healthy person I am becoming.

The same rules hold true for holidays, they come every year. When I look at my calendar there is not a single month that doesn't have at least three celebrations of some type. Whether it be the big holidays like Easter, Christmas, and such or birthdays. It seems there is rarely a week that there is not some challenge for manipulating healthy eating choices. I think by coming to grips with this idea, it makes the event easier to treat as a healthy eating opportunity and not a Last Supper. Make compromises with the celebrations, and put forth some activity planning. All events do not have to be centered around food. Change some of the traditions of your family. Instead of a nap after Thanksgiving. What about a walk around your neighborhood.

Week SIXTEEN and beyond….

Maintenance

I am thrilled with my weight loss and those that have followed this program and became healthier people by reaching a healthy BMI (Body Mass Index). I am ecstatic that those who have lost the weight really understand how to maintain the loss. This is the overall goal of this program. The key is simple. You have to be aware of your weight on a weekly basis. In one of the corporate meetings I do, the owner of the company who maintains his goal weight beautifully uses his belt as an indicator for when to cut back calories and increase activity. I love learning from those around me and his tip is a good one.

In order to lose a pound a week on this program, the goal is to reduce 500 calories a day. In a weeks time you have reduced 3500 calories and that is one pound. When you reach your healthy weight, you have probably increased your activity to the point you can add back the 500 calories that were in the red and maintain your loss. The weeks following reaching your goal are very important. You should continue to write down everything you are eating, and honestly track your calories adding back the 500 to your day. Weigh yourself weekly and adjust the calorie needs based on the scale, if you have a gain, cut back calories. If you are still losing add a few more calories. There is no magic number and this phase will take a little tweaking to get the numbers to balance with the scale.

Then if you continue to monitor what your weight is and find the scale creeping up, go back on the weight loss plan and cut the 500 calories from your day's choices. The important part of this phase is self monitoring.

Weight does fluctuate according to the choices we make and the weight and content of the foods we are choosing. I give myself a 2 pound lead way on each side of my goal weight. As long as I am 2 pounds below or above my goal I stay on the maintenance plan. If I go beyond the two pound goal I immediately go back on the weight loss program. A pound is easily lost but it can multiply so quickly to so much more. So make a pack with yourself to not go beyond your threshold.

Only one pound

Hello, do you know me? If you don't you should I um a pound of fat and I'm the happiest pound of fat that you would ever want to meet. Want to know why? It's because no one ever wants to lose me. I'm only a pound, just a pound!

Everyone wants to lose three, five, or ten pounds, but never only one. So I just stick around and happily keep you fat. Then I ever so slyly, add myself to ten, fifteen or twenty pounds or even more. Yes, It is fun being only one pound of fat. So when you weigh in keep right on saying, "Oh I only lost one pound." (as if it were a terrible thing) For you see, if you do this, you'll encourage others to keep me around because they'll think I'm not worth losing.

And, I love being around you, your arms, thighs, waist, every part of you. Happy Days!!! After all, I'm ONLY ONE POUND OF FAT!

Author unknown

It is very important to make journaling your food choices your own, If your prefer to list your intake on the computer, do so. If you purchase a notebook and use that, Great. If you use a napkin before you eat that also works. Please put pen to paper. And before you eat anything, pause and think about what you are doing. Make certain you are in control and write down the food and the calories associated with the choice. So many members tell me this is the secret to their success and they have decided that maybe they do not want the choice once they really thought about it.

Find the system that means the most to you and commit to sixteen weeks of journaling your choice.

If you Bite it, write it….

Before you pick up your eating utensil, grab your pencil.

Now, that you have kept a journal, you have a better idea of your choices and where some changes can be made. Take a few minutes and review the tips listed earlier and ask your self-what changes you are willing to make on a continuous basis to reach a healthy weight and Body Mass Index. Remember there are three ways to lose weight. You can consume fewer calories, you can exert more energy by increasing your activity, or you can raise your resting metabolic rate through increasing muscle mass. A deficit of 250-500 calories a day will yield 1/2 to 1 pound of weight loss a week. Ask yourself what you are willing to do to improve your health. Can you increase your activity? Are you willing to lighten up your menu? Will you add more fruits and vegetables to your diet? Will you limit added sugars and alcohol?

My COMMITMENT

In 1 year I want to have a _____ pound weight loss. To accomplish this I am willing to commit to adding 16 weeks of healthy tips to my life. One step at a time I will reach my goal weight.

Signature_____ Date_____

Living Healthy, Living Well ....

Lose weight in a healthy way.

Ignore fad diets and concentrate on healthy eating.

Deal with stress in nonfood ways.

Add physical activity every day.

Eat breakfast every day.

Do not skip meals.

Include a variety of foods.

Weigh one time a week and keep a record of progress.

Set realistic goals.

Be flexible.

Keep Health a priority.

WEIGHT CHART FOR 12-month goal.

Today's weight_____

10% goal_____

Date _____Weight _____Pounds lost_____

Date _____Weight _____Pounds lost_____

Date___ _____Weight_ _____Pounds lost_____

Date _____Weight _____Pounds lost_____

Date _____Weight _____Pounds lost_____

Date _____Weight_ _____Pounds lost_____

Date _____Weight _____Pounds lost_____

Date _____Weight_ _____Pounds lost_____

Date _____Weight _____Pounds lost_____

Date _____Weight_ _____Pounds lost_____

Date _____Weight _____Pounds lost_____

Date___ _____Weight_ _____Pounds lost_____

My weight loss journey was a two-year learning experience. The maintenance continues, I have not reverted to old unhealthy ways. I have adopted several new recipes. My favorite food choices are included here to aid in your new lifestyle changes.

Favorite low calorie beverages

Alpine Sugar-free Spiced Cider

Celestial Seasonings teas

Sugar free hot chocolate (Nestle, Swiss Miss)

Tropicana Sugar free orange-aide

V8 Diet Splash

V8

Favorite low calorie Snacks

Blue Bunny frozen novelties -no sugar added

Fat free Pringles = 15 chips are one serving

Jell-O- sugar free Jell-O and puddings

Laughing Cow light cheese bites

Tootsie pop

All Bran cereal bars

Barbara's Puffins cereal bas

Kellogg's All-Bran cereal bars

Jolly time 94% fat free popcorn

Sugar free Jolly ranchers

Gen soy= soy crisps- 25 is one serving

Splenda flavor blends for coffee

Vita muffins (freezer section of Grocery store)

Dannon light & fit yogurt

No Purge giant fudgy bars

Smuckers sugar free preserves and whole grain English muffin

Light ruffles potato chips= 15 chips or 1 ounce

Reduced fat string cheese

Mini teddy grams- 53 is one serving

ANY FRUIT

Fresh sliced veggies

Enjoy the journey, small changes yield big results.

Now, you have an understanding of the link between a 3500 reduction in calories to burn or lose one pound. Your next step is to learn to burn those calories in the most efficient way possible. Remember the sneaky steps, find a place to work them in on a daily basis, and maybe you can start to schedule 30 minutes of activity on most days, each step is improving your general health.

Nutrition 101

Good nutrition, exercise and the way you think about food is the key. Chose foods rich in complex carbohydrates, fiber, vitamins and low in fat. Carbohydrates are very important to the daily diet. It is recommended that 60% of your daily calories come from complex carbohydrates. Those include legumes (dry beans and peas), breads, starchy vegetables, cereals and pastas, fruits and vegetables.

Protein is known as the building blocks for our body, because of it's ability to build tissue. It is very important to include protein at every meal.

Fat is the most concentrated source of calories. You must have the essential fatty acids to use the fat soluble vitamins (Vitamins A, D, E, and K). A high fat diet is associated with heart disease and some cancers. You need to reduce the fat in your diet. There are different types of fat in your diet and some are healthier that others. Saturated fat is the fat we get from dairy and meat. It is a good idea to limit total fat and saturated fat in your diet. Monounsaturated fat is found in olive, canola oil and some nuts. This type of fat helps to lower cholesterol and should be included in your diet. Polyunsaturated fat is found in vegetable and corn oils and should be used in limited amounts. To reduce the risk of some diseases your daily calories should be less than 30% fat.

Fiber is the nondigestable part of a plant. According to medical professionals, it may prevent heart disease and some cancers. Eating a high fiber diet should be part of a healthy diet. It is recommended that you include 25-30g of fiber in your diet daily.

In order to get the adequate vitamins and minerals it is important to eat a variety of foods. When you are aware of your current eating pattern, it is easy to incorporate small changes. If you follow these guidelines, just like running your car on premium gasoline, you will be running your body as efficiently as possible.

Favorite Recipes

Asparagus Omelet's

(Serves 4 @ 98 cal.)

You can use broccoli instead...

1 large egg
5 large egg whites
1 Tbsp. fresh chives (or freeze dried)
2 Tbsp. cold water
Dash of black pepper
2 Tbsp. unsalted margarine
1/4 cup finely chopped, cooked asparagus or broccoli
1/4 cup finely chopped mushrooms
1/4 cup finely chopped tomato
1/4 cup minced parsley

In a medium-sized bowl, combine egg, egg whites, chives, water and pepper.

Whisk just enough to mix lightly. Melt 1/2 Tbsp of the margarine in a heavy 7" skillet over moderately high heat. Add 1/4 each of the asparagus and mushrooms and cook, stirring, for 1 minute. Add 1/4 of the egg mixture (about 1/2 cup) and shake the skillet over the heat, stirring, for 30 seconds, then let the omelet cook, undisturbed, for 30 seconds more, or until the edges and bottom are set. With a spatula, either fold the omelet in half or roll it to the edge of the pan and invert it onto a heated plate. Make 3 more omelets in the same way. Top with chopped tomato and parsley and sprinkle with parsley.

VARIATION:

Herb-Mushroom Omelet: Omit the asparagus and add 1 Tbsp. minced fresh dill, oregano, basil, sage and tarragon to the egg mixture just before cooking.

(1 g Fiber; 98 Calories; 7 g Fat; 2 g Carb)

Broccoli Italian

(Serves 6 @ 50 cal.)

You can serve it with some pasta, too.
3 cups broccoli
1/2 cup thinly sliced green onions
4 tsp. olive oil
4 garlic cloves, minced
2 Tbsp. lemon juice
1/2 tsp. salt
1/4 tsp. pepper
2 large fresh mushrooms, sliced

Steam broccoli until crisp-tender. While it is cooking, sauté onions and mushroom in oil over medium heat until barely tender. Add garlic and cook for 30 seconds longer.

Reduce heat. Add broccoli, lemon juice, salt and pepper.

Toss to coat.

(1 g Fiber; 50 calories; 3 g Fat; 5 g Carb.)

Jell-O Salad

(Serves 4 at Basically 0 Calories!)

Add 2-3 Tablespoons each of finely grated carrots, finely grated cabbage, finely chopped celery and chopped, seeded cucumbers. Blend with the jello (at the moment when you add the cold water)

Refrigerate until firm, then add 1 tsp. of Cool Whip Free. This is delicious by itself or served with cottage cheese.

Jell-o especially sugar free is one of those fun foods that you always want to have on hand. It is fat free and a good protein source. I love to mix it and add to cool whip, pour in a pie pan and freeze. Yummy!

Italian Rice 'n Beans

(Serves 4 @ 330 cal.)

1 1/2 cups cooked rice
1 Tbsp. olive oil
1 large onion, chopped
2 clove garlic, minced
1 can low sodium tomatoes
2 medium carrots, peeled & sliced
1 medium zucchini, sliced
1/2 cup water
1 large stalk celery, chopped
Basil (1 Tbsp. fresh or 1 tsp dried)
1 tsp. dried oregano
Dash of black pepper
2 cups kidney beans, cooked & drained
1/4 cup Parmesan cheese.

Heat olive oil in a heavy skillet. Sauté onion and garlic until soft, about 5 minutes. Add water, tomatoes, carrots, celery, basil, oregano, and pepper. Bring to a boil. Add a little more water if necessary. Reduce the heat and simmer for 15 minutes. Stir in kidney beans and cook for another 5 minutes to heat through.

Divide rice into 4 servings. Divide veggies into 4 servings and serve over the rice. Sprinkle each with Parmesan Cheese.

(2 g Dietary Fiber; 330 calories; 6 g Fat; 58 g Carb)

Dreamy Creamy Potatoes

(Serves 4 at 100 Cal.)

1 1/2 pounds russet potatoes, peeled and cut into 2-inch pieces
1 tablespoon olive or canola oil
3 tablespoons reduced-fat sour cream or plain nonfat yogurt
1/8 teaspoon salt
1/8 teaspoon freshly ground pepper

Place potatoes in a large saucepan and add enough water to cover. Bring to a boil over medium heat and simmer until potatoes are fork tender, 20 to 30 minutes. Drain potatoes, reserving 1 cup cooking liquid. Press potatoes through a ricer or mash in the saucepan.

Stir in oil, sour cream, salt, and pepper until well blended. Gradually stir in some of the reserved cooking liquid until the potatoes become creamy and smooth.

(2 g Dietary Fiber; 125 Calories; 4 g Fat; 20 g Carb)

Baked Apple

(Serves 6 at 100 Cal.)

6 medium tart apples, cored and peal 1/3 of the way down
1 lemon, cut in half
1 tsp. ground cinnamon
2 tsp. brown sugar substitute water
6 gingersnaps, crushed

Place apples in a microwave-safe dish. Rub the pared flesh of each apple with a cut side of the lemon. Squeeze juice of both halves over the apples. Sprinkle each with cinnamon and brown sugar substitute. Fill the dish with water 1/3 way up the sides of the apples. Cover with plastic wrap, venting at one edge.

(3 g Dietary Fiber; 104 calories; 1 g Fat; 25 g Carb)

Fish 'n Chips

(Serves 4 @ 240 cal.)

2 large baking potatoes, scrubbed and cut lengthwise into 16 spears each
2 Tbsp. Old Bay Seasoning
1/2 cup yellow cornmeal
4 (4-oz.) cod fillets

Preheat oven to 425. Spray potatoes with Pam. Place in a large zip-close plastic bag with 1 Tbsp. of the Old Bay.

Seal the bag and shake to coat. Transfer to a large baking sheet lined with foil and lightly sprayed with Pam. In the same plastic bag, combine cornmeal and remaining Old Bay; shake to mix. Spray the fillets with Pam and shake in bag to coat. Place in a single layer on the baking sheet with the potatoes. Bake until the fish is golden brown and flakes easily and the potato spears are fork-tender, about 25 minutes.

(3 g Dietary Fiber; 240 Calories; 1 g Fat; 33 g Carb

Sour Cream Enchiladas

(Serves 4 @ 330 cal.)

1 (8-oz.) container light sour cream
1 (8-oz.) container nonfat plain yogurt
1 10 3/4-oz.) can condensed 99%-fat- free cream of chicken soup with 1/3 less salt
1 (4-oz.) can diced green chilies
12 (6 or 7-inch) white corn or flour tortillas
4 oz. (1 cup) shredded 1/3-less-fat Cheddar cheese
1 1/2 cups chopped cooked chicken
1/4 cup sliced green onions

Heat oven to 350°F. Spray 13x9-inch (3-quart) baking dish with nonstick cooking spray. In medium bowl, combine sour cream, yogurt, soup and chilies; mix well. Spoon about 3 tablespoons sour cream mixture down center of each tortilla. Reserve 1/4 cup of the cheese; sprinkle tortillas with remaining cheese, chicken and onions. Roll up; place in sprayed dish. Spoon remaining sour cream mixture over tortillas. Cover with foil. Bake at 350°F. for 25 to 30 minutes or until hot and bubbly. Remove foil; sprinkle with reserved 1/4 cup cheese. Bake uncovered for an additional 5 minutes or until cheese is melted. If desired, garnish with shredded lettuce and chopped tomatoes.

(3 g Dietary Fiber; 350 Calories; 11 g Fat)

Chicken Tacos

(Serves 8 at 210 Cal.)

8 whole taco shells, broken up
1 and 1/2 cup chopped, cooked chicken breast
1/2 c onions, chopped
4 ozs cheddar cheese, shredded
1 c bell peppers, chopped
6 cups iceberg lettuce, crisped and torn

Dressing:

3/4 c salsa
1/4 cup low fat mayonnaise or Miracle Whip Free
1 Tbsp. taco seasoning mix

Blend salsa, mayo and taco seasoning mix. Toss with all ingredients.

(2 g Dietary Fiber; 210 Calories; 7 g Fat; 16 g Carb)

Chicken 'n Artichokes

(4 servings at 260 Cal.)

1/2 Tbsp. Olive Oil
4 (1/2 pound) skinless boneless chicken breasts halves
4 small red potatoes, thinly sliced
6 kalamata olives, pitted and quartered
12 canned artichoke quarters (packed in water)
1 Tbsp. chopped basil
1/8 tsp. rosemary

Heat a nonstick skillet. Add oil. Slightly heat, then add the chicken breasts in a single layer. Sear until browned, about 2 minutes on each side.

Remove to a plate. In the same skillet, Add potatoes and cook, stirring occasionally until they begin to brown. Stir in olives, artichokes and basil, then return chicken to pan. Reduce the heat to the lowest setting possible, cover; and cook until the chicken is cooked through and the potatoes are well-browned. (About 5 minutes with a stir at 2-3 minutes.)

(2 g Dietary Fiber, 260 calories, 1 g Fat, 24 g Carbs)

Fiesta Skillet Supper

(Serves 8 at 252 Cal.

1 pound ground turkey breast or extra lean ground beef
1 envelope taco seasoning mix
2 cups salsa
4 cups tomato sauce or juice
1 15-oz. can black beans, drained
2 cups instant rice

Spray a large Dutch oven with Pam. Cook the turkey and taco seasoning mix together in the prepared pan over medium heat until fully cooked. Add the salsa, tomato sauce and black beans. Bring to a boil. Add the rice, making sure the rice is covered with liquid. Add a bit of water if necessary. Turn off the heat and stir. Cover and let sit for 5 minutes.

Enjoy with a salad or a bit of sliced fruit.

(4 g Dietary Fiber; 252 Calories; 1 g Fat; 55 g Carb)

Fall Day Beans (last picnic of year)

(Serves 7 at 270 calories - 3/4 cup per serving)

2 (15 oz cans of pork and beans)
2 cups finely chopped onion
1 cup finely chopped green bell pepper
1/2 cup ketchup
1/2 cup firmly packed brown sugar
1/2 cup molasses
1 tsp. barbeque smoked seasoning (i.e. liquid smoke)
Dash of hot sauce

Preheat oven to 425. Spray a 2 quart casserole with Pam. Combine all ingredients and pour into a 2 quart casserole that has been sprayed with Pam. Bake, uncovered, for 40 minutes, or until bubbly.

(8 g Dietary Fiber; 270 Calories; 1.5 g Fat; 62 g Carb)

Watermelon Salad

(Serves 6 at 55 Calories)

6 Cups watermelon, peeled and cubed
1/2 small red onion; thinly sliced
1/3 cup apple cider vinegar
2-3 tablespoons mint leaves; chopped
1/2 teaspoon freshly ground pepper

Chill melon before preparing, especially if it is very ripe.

Combine all ingredients gently.

(1 g Dietary Fiber; 55 Calories; 0 g Fat; 13 g Carbs)

Variation. This yummy dressing can be used with other fruits and veggies. Another favorite is broccoli and raisins. Be creative. I would love to hear what you find that is delicious.

Cream of Cauliflower Soup

(Makes 8 at 76 Calories)

2 Tsp. olive oil
1 cup chopped onion
1 head cauliflower, broken into florets
3 cups low-sodium chicken broth
3/4 cup evaporated fat-free milk (or 2% milk)
1/4 tsp. freshly grated nutmeg
Salt and pepper to taste

Sauté onions in oil in a nonstick skillet until tender. About 5 minutes. Add cauliflower and broth. Bring to a boil. Lower heat to medium and cook until cauliflower can be easily mashed. About 10 minutes. Transfer in batches to a blender and puree, pouring puree mixture into another soup pot. Over low heat stir milk into pureed mixture. Add seasonings and serve. Very pretty garnished with chopped fresh parsley.

(Six 1 cup servings: 3 g Dietary Fiber; 85 calories; 3 g Fat; 10 g Carb)

Apple Crisp

(Serves 2 at 200 Calories)

2 Empire or other firm apples, peeled, cored and thinly sliced
1/4 cup quick-cooking oatmeal
2 Tbsp. firmly packed light brown sugar
1 1/2 Tbsp. all-purpose flour
1/2 tsp. cinnamon
Pinch of nutmeg
2 tsp. olive oil

Steam sliced apples in a vegetable steamer until barely tender. Drain and place in a small, oven-proof baking dish that has been sprayed with Pam. While apples are cooking, blend remaining ingredients by cutting with knives or scissors until it resembles crumbs. Sprinkle topping over fruit and bake for 7-10 minutes at 350. Keep an eye on it so it doesn't get too toasty.

(4 g Dietary Fiber; 200 Calories; 3 g Total Fat; 44 g Carbs.)

Chicken Broccoli Stir-Fry

(Serves 4 @ 225 cal.)

---

1 Tbsp. cornstarch
1/4 Cup Dijon mustard
1 Tbsp. reduced sod. Soy Sauce
2 Tbsp. olive oil
1/2 pound boneless chicken breast
8 medium scallion, sliced thin
7 cups broccoli florets
1/2 cup shredded red cabbage
1/2 medium carrot, shredded.

In medium bowl, whisk 1/4 cup water with cornstarch until smooth. Whisk in mustard, soy sauce and honey, set aside. Place large nonstick skillet over medium heat and heat for 30 seconds. add oil and heat 30 seconds more. Add chicken and scallions, cook, stirring constantly 3-4 minutes, until chicken is beginning to turn golden. Add veggies and 1 cup water. Reduce heat to low and simmer, covered, until chicken is cooked through and vegetables are crisp--tender. Add prepared sauce and cook, stirring gently for 3-5 minutes, until thickened. Divide into 4 servings, and enjoy!

(9 g Dietary Fiber; 225 Calories; 6 g Total Fat; 22 G Protein)

Cucumber and Sweet Pepper Salad

(Serves 4 at 40 Cal.)

1/4 cup plain low-fat yogurt
2 tsp. olive, sesame or peanut oil
3/4 tsp. cider vinegar
1/2 tsp. minced fresh ginger
1/4 tsp. ground cumin
1/4 tsp. ground coriander
1 large cucumber,
1 small sweet red pepper

Prepare cucumber by peeling, halving lengthwise, then seeding and cutting into matchstick strips. Core, seed and cut red pepper into matchstick strips. In a medium-sized bowl, combine the yogurt, oil, vinegar, ginger, cumin and coriander. Add the cucumber and red pepper and toss well. Cover and chill in the refrigerator for several hours to blend flavors.

(1 g Dietary Fiber; 40 calories; 3 g Fat; 4 g Carb)

Orange Breakfast Cookie

(Makes 24 cookies at 135 calories each)

3/4 cup margarine
1 cup dark brown sugar
1 egg
1/4 cup skim milk
1/4 cup orange juice concentrate
1 cup all-purpose flour
1 tsp. baking powder
3/4 tsp. salt
1/4 cup wheat germ
1/4 tsp. cinnamon
1 1/2 cup oats
1 cup raisins
1/2 cup chopped walnuts

Preheat oven to 350. Cream margarine, brown sugar and eggs. Add milk. Stir in orange juice concentrate. In a separate bowl combine dry ingredients and add to creamed mixture. Add oats, raisins and walnuts. Mix well. Drop by heaping teaspoons onto cookie sheets sprayed with Pam, leaving plenty of room for spreading during cooking. Flatten balls with the bottom of a drinking glass that has been sprayed with pam. Bake 10-12 minutes.

(1.5 g Dietary Fiber; 135 Calories; 5 g Fat)

Single serve Breakfast Bar

This recipe make ONE large cookie:

1/3 cup oatmeal
1 T flour
1/3 cup Fat Free Dry Milk
1/4 teaspoon baking powder
1/4 teaspoon cinnamon (a little less if you want)
2 T splenda
1/4 cup sugar free applesauce
2 Tablespoons Raisins (optional)

Mix all ingredients.

Spray cookie sheet with Pam and spread out with the back of a spoon. Bake at 350 for 10 minutes. Turn over with a spatula and bake for another 5-10 minutes.

Greek Lentil Salad

(Serves 4 @ 225 cal.)

2 cups water
1 cup dried lentils
1/2 tsp. salt
1 bay leaf
1 cup diced cucumber
1/2 cup diced celery
1/4 cup diced red onion
2 Tbsp. white wine vinegar
4 tsp. Dijon mustard
1/2 cup crumbled feta cheese

Combine first four ingredients in a medium saucepan. Bring to a boil, cover, reduce heat and simmer for 25 minutes, or until tender. Drain. Discard bay leaf. Combine the cooked lentils, with cucumber, celery, and onion in a bowl. Whisk together orange juice, vinegar and mustard in a small bowl. Toss with veggies and lentils. Stir in cheese. Cover and chill well (at least two hours) to blend flavors.

(6.1 g Fiber; 225 calories; 3.9 g Fat; 32.5 g Carb)

Honey Stuffed Sweet Potatoes

(Serves 2 at 124 Cal.)

Buy some sweet potatoes and make this now! Then savor the memory and make it again for Thanksgiving.

Scrub one medium/large (about 8 oz.) sweet potato. Wrap in foil and bake at 400 until tender (about 40 minutes) Let the potato cool until you can handle it. Cut it in half lengthwise, and scoop out the pulp, leaving the shell intact. Add 1 tsp. honey and a dash of cinnamon and nutmeg. Whip until fluffy with your electric mixer. Spoon half of the mixture back into each shell and reheat in either oven or microwave.

(4 g Fiber; 124 calories;.5 g Fat; 25 g Carb)

Grilled Sweet Potatoes

(Serves 2 at 190 Calories)

1 large sweet potato (about 12 oz.)
2 tsp. Dijon style mustard
2 tsp. honey
2 tsp. olive oil
1 tsp. snipped fresh rosemary (or 1/2 tsp. dried)
Freshly ground black pepper.

Pierce potato and cook in microwave for 6-8 minutes until tender, but still firm. Let cool, then peel and slice.

In a separate bowl mix remaining ingredients. Place potatoes on grill and brush with honey-mustard. Cook for 2-3 minutes, turn and brush again with remaining sauce.

(4 g Dietary Fiber; 190 calories; 5 g Fat; 36 g Carb)

Apples with Ginger and Snow Peas

(Makes 4 servings)

2 tsps olive oil
2 tbsps peeled fresh ginger, finely slivered
3 cloves garlic, minced
1 pound snow peas; remove the strings
2 crisp red apples, unpeeled, cut into thin wedges (Fuji are great)
1/4 to 1/2 tsp salt

In a large nonstick skillet heat the oil over low heat. Add the ginger and garlic and cook a couple of minutes, until tender. Add the snow peas, apples and salt to the skillet and cook until peas are crisp-tender, about 7 minutes, stirring frequently. Divide into four servings (about 2/3 cup).

110 Calories, 2.5 g Total Fat, 300 mg Sodium, 5 g Dietary Fiber, 0 mg Cholesterol, 20 g Carbohydrate, 3 g protein

Toasted Angel Food Cake

(8 servings at 285 calories each)

2 1/2 cups sliced nectarines* (about 1 pound)
2 1/2 cups sliced plums (about 1 pound)
1 cup raspberries
1/4 cup sugar
1/4 cup cranberry-raspberry drink
1 teaspoon lemon juice
Cooking spray
8 (1/2 -inch-thick) slices angel food cake

Combine the first 6 ingredients in a large bowl; cover and marinate the fruit mixture 30 minutes in refrigerator, stirring occasionally. Place a large nonstick griddle or nonstick skillet coated with cooking spray over medium-high heat until hot. Arrange the angel food cake slices in a single layer on pan, and cook for 2 minutes on each side or until the cake slices are toasted. Place 1 cake slice on each of 8 plates, and top each slice with 3/4 cup marinated fruit mixture.

*A pound of peaches can be used instead of nectarines.

(1.5 g Dietary Fiber; 285 Calories; 3 g Fat)

TIPS FOR LOSING WEIGHT

1. Good things come in small packages. Here's a trick for staying satisfied without consuming large portions: Chop high-calorie foods like cheese and chocolate into smaller pieces. It will seem like you're getting more than you actually are.

2. Get "water-wise." Make a habit of reaching for a glass of water instead of a high-fat snack. It will help your overall health as well as your waistline. So drink up! Add some zest to your six, eight ounce glasses a day with a twist of lemon or lime.

3. Herb it up. Stock up your spice rack, and start growing a small herb garden in your kitchen window. Spices and herbs add fantastic flavor to foods without adding fat or calories.

4. Slim down your soup. Make a big batch of soup and refrigerate it before you eat it. As it cools, the fat will rise to the top and can be skimmed off the surface.

5. Doggie-bag that dinner. At restaurants that you know serve large portions, ask the waiter to put half of your main course in a take-home box before bringing it to your table. Putting the food away before you start your meal will help you practice portion control. Always wear fitted clothes when you are dining out. The more comfortable your slacks or jeans are the more apt you will be to over eat.

6. Listen to your cravings. If you're craving something sweet, eat something sweet—just opt for a healthier nosh (like fruit) instead of a high-calorie one like ice cream. The same goes for crunchy cravings—for example, try air-popped popcorn instead of high-fat chips. It's just smart substitution!

7. Ease your way into produce. If you're new to eating lots of fruits and vegetables, start slowly. Just add them to the foods you already enjoy. Pile salad veggies into your sandwiches, or add fruit to your cereal.

8. Look for high-fat hints. Do you need an easy way to identify high-calorie meals? Keep an eye out for these words: au gratin, Parmigianino, tempura, Alfredo, creamy and carbonara, and enjoy them in moderation.

9. Don't multi-task while you eat. If you're working, reading or watching TV while you eat, you won't be paying attention to what's going into your mouth—and you won't be enjoying every bite. Every time you have a meal, sit down. Chew slowly and pay attention to flavors and textures. You'll enjoy your food more and eat less.

10. Taste something new. Broaden your food repertoire—you may find you like more healthy foods than you knew. Try a new fruit or vegetable (ever had plantain, starfruit or papaya?).

11. Leave something on your plate at every meal. One bite of bagel, half your sandwich, the bun from your burger. See if you still feel satisfied eating just a bit less.

12. Get to know your portion sizes. It's easy to underestimate how much you're eating. Don't just estimate things—make sure. Ask how much is in a serving, read the fine print on labels, measure your food. And learn portion equivalents: One serving of pasta, for instance, should be around the size of your fist.

13. Don't give up dips. If you love creamy dips and sauces, don't cut them out of your food plan completely. Just use low-fat soft cheese and mayonnaise instead of the full fat stuff.

14. Make a healthy substitution. Learn to swap healthier foods for their less-healthy counterparts. Find a substitution that works for you: Use skim or low-fat milk instead of whole milk; try whole-wheat bread instead of white.

Milk

Drinking whole milk cappuccinos and lattes will use your daily *calories* up quickly. Use fat-free or low-fat milk instead, and look for flavored coffees or sugar-free syrups to improve that cup of java.

Make smoothies by blending fat-free milk with low-fat or fat-free yogurt, a banana, frozen strawberries and honey to taste.

Use low-fat milk when making mashed potatoes.

Rice pudding is just as nice made with low-fat milk. Add flavor with cinnamon, and sprinkle the top with nutmeg.

Bread

Instead of serving bread with soup, add a tablespoon of bulgur wheat or a 1/2 cup of brown rice to your homemade recipe.

As a change-up from bread sandwiches, generously fill

whole-wheat tortilla wraps with chunks of fresh-cooked chicken, coriander, lettuce and red pepper, adding a teaspoon of low-fat mayonnaise.

Potatoes

Switch to sweet potatoes or yams. Cut up the sweet potatoes and roast in a hot oven for 30 minutes, sprinkled with sea salt and a little olive oil, or lightly boil and mash with a small amount of butter.

Boil some couscous to fluff up and serve with grilled fish or meat.

Filling Fruits

Dried fruits come into their own in the winter months and make excellent after-dinner desserts. Put dried apricots, prunes and pineapple chunks in a pan and cover with a little orange juice. Bring to a boil, then let stand for 20 minutes so the fruit can absorb the juices. Sprinkle with a little cinnamon and serve with spoonful of low-fat yogurt.

Poach peeled pears in a low-calorie fruity cordial with one cinnamon stick until tender. Serve with low-fat or fat-free yogurt.

Cheese

Get into the habit of buying low-fat varieties. Keep a tub of low-fat or fat-free cottage cheese on hand to mix in with fresh fruit or sprinkle with Splenda and cinnamon for a sweet treat.

Sprinkle a teaspoon or two of freshly grated Parmesan over your pasta, a little of its big-hitting flavor goes a long way.

Poultry and Meat

Trim off fat before cooking.

Always roast chicken on a rack in a roasting tin, so the saturated fat drains off.

If you plan to marinate the meat, use lean strips of pork or beef.

When making casseroles, cook them the day before, so as it cools you can skim any fat off the top before reheating.

15. Bring lunch to work tomorrow. Packing lunch will help you control your portion sizes. It also provides a good alternative to restaurants and takeaways, where making healthy choices every day can be challenging (not to mention expensive).

16. Have some dessert. You don't have to deny yourself all the time. Have a treat that brings you pleasure, but this time enjoy it guilt-free be—sure you're practicing portion control, and compensate for your indulgence by exercising a little more or by skipping your afternoon snack.

17. Ask for what you need. Tell your mother-in-law you don't want seconds. Ask your other half to stop bringing you chocolates. Speak up for the place with great salads when your co-workers are picking a restaurant for lunch. Whatever you need to do to succeed at weight loss, ask for it—make yourself a priority and assert yourself. Many times others are needing a healthy nudge and your choice can become contagious.

18. Improve your treadmill technique. When walking on a treadmill, don't grip the rails. It's fine to touch them for balance, but you shouldn't have to hold on. If you do, that might be a signal you should lower the intensity level.

19.... get moving. Here's an easy way to fit in exercise with your kids: Buy a set of 1 lb weights and play a round of Simon Says — you do it with the weights, they do it without. They'll love it! And remember to pick them up during TV commercials.

20. Make the most of your walks. If your walking routine has become too easy, increase your effort by finding hills. Just be sure to tackle them at the beginning of your walk, when you have energy to spare. You can even remember to bring those hand weights along with you.

21. Holiday tip Shop 'til you drop...pounds! Add a workout to your shopping sessions by walking around the mall before your start spending. And try walking up the escalator — getting to your destination faster will be an added bonus.

22. Walk an extra 100 steps at work. Adding even a little extra exercise to your daily routine can boost your weight loss. Today, take the stairs instead of the elevator, or stroll down the hall to talk to a co-worker instead of sending an email or calling. Move the trash can away from your desk.

23. Brush your teeth after every meal and snack. This will be a signal to your mouth — and your mind — that it's time to stop eating. Brushing will also give your mouth a nice fresh taste that you'll be disinclined to ruin with a random chip. At work, keep a toothbrush with a cover and toothpaste in your desk drawer. If munching while you prepare dinner is a problem, brush your teeth before you begin the meal prep.

24. Clean your closet. First, it's great exercise. Second, it's an important step in changing your attitude. Get rid of all the clothes that make you look or feel bad. Throw out anything that's too big—don't give yourself the option of ever fitting into those clothes again. Move the smaller clothes up to the front to help motivate you. Soon, you'll be fitting into those too-tight jeans you couldn't bear to part with.

25. Take your measurements. You might not like your stats now, but you'll be glad you wrote them down when you see how many inches you've lost. It's also another way to measure your success, instead of just looking at the scale. Sometimes even when the numbers on the scale aren't going down, the measurements on your body are. Even plan to wear a belt, moving to another notch is motivating.

The last portion of this tool addresses some questions that I believe takes this journey and makes it permanent. Why did you buy this book, are you enrolled in a nutrition class and want to change your waist size? Did you doctor tell you your blood pressure was elevated and you need to get to a healthier weight? Honestly, have this conversation with yourself and determine why you want to lose weight. Is it for a special event, a reunion or wedding? Is it for the summer, with bathing suits and sleeveless tops? Or are you in for the life time? If you are changing your habits for a short time to lose weight for a reason or season. I urge you to reconsider. If many of you calculate the pounds you have lost and gained many times with interest. You have probably lost as much weight as I have. It is just my last time at this job was the last for me. The 106 pounds that I lost, I never want to lose any of them again. If you have 5, 10, 25 or 100 pounds as your goal, and you spend your time working toward that goal, reaching that goal and celebrating that goal; shouldn't it be for a lifetime. Well many times before the single pound gain soon became all the weight you had lost and you were back to the job of getting to your ideal weight again. This time please make the changes slowly, shooting for one pound a week, average. Habits develop over a 16 to 20 week period, when I describe how making healthy habits without making a conscious effort happened with me, I think it was so subtle I could not recognize it. Kind of like when you drive to work or school, you take the same route, and before long you get into the car in the morning and start your trip and without recognizing all the familiar turns and stops, then you are there. You pass the same buildings and may not even recall them, you probably don't recall turning on the switch, or putting the car into drive either. You did all those tasks without making a conscious effort. The last commute you made on familiar ground was with less conscious effort than the first time you did it.

Thank you for putting forth the resources to acquire this material. I would like to touch on the cost and benefits of making healthy choices. Many people tell me they recognize a huge increase in the cost of healthier options. Here are some tips for combating the cost. And remember it is very difficult to put a price on being healthier. How much would you spend to get your health back if it were failing?

Budget tips for healthy living:

Make a meal plan for the week. Check your grocery's ad circular, and plan your recipes around it. Make a shopping list based on those recipes, checking what you already have so that you don't purchase unnecessary duplicates.

Look for spices and canned goods in the ethnic food aisle; they tend to be different brands than those found elsewhere in the store, at cheaper prices.

If you have children, hire a babysitter. What you save on junk food and impulse purchases will more than pay for the babysitter.

If you shop at a butcher, look for 10 lb. combination packs of meat and poultry that they need to move; freeze what you don't immediately need. Regular grocery stores often offer value packs; break into 1 lb quantities, wrap each in plastic wrap, then package in ziplock bags and freeze for later.

Double recipes, especially if using bulk or sale ingredients; freeze half for later.

Shop farmer's markets for fruit and vegetables.

Buy produce that is in season.

Consider buying a CSA (community supported agriculture) share:

Consider cheap non-meat sources. Eat high-protein beans and grains such as kidney beans, black beans, and chickpeas, paired with brown rice, quinoa and barley.

Rely on bags of frozen and canned vegetables when possible. They are a convenience that is surprisingly the same price (or less) as the fresh counterpart, with less spoilage issues.

Buy grains in bulk, from the bins at your health food store. These are cheaper than packaged.

Eat out less often. A family of four spends, at a minimum, $45 for one fast food meal out. For $45 you can buy at least 12 chicken breasts, 6 cartons of broth, 6 heads of romaine lettuce, and 6 boxes of whole-wheat pasta.

Look for cuts of meat that are marked down for sale that day. If they are large cuts, then divide them into one-meal sized portions and freeze them for later, or use them that day.

Buy boneless, skinless chicken breasts and thighs in bulk. They're great for using in salads, soups, and just for grilling. As soon as you get them home, throw most of them on the grill. You'll have grilled chicken to use the rest of the week.

Bone-in chicken is cheaper and sometimes more flavorful than boneless and skinless chicken. Just remove the skin prior to eating.

Buy the store brand when it's not a compromise on quality. It's always cheaper and often you can't tell the difference. Use coupons for whatever brand names are necessary/desirable.

Waste nothing. NOTHING. Freeze bits of tomato sauce, tomato paste, broth, etc. for later and then wind up using them. Freeze about-to-spoil fresh fruit in bite-sized chunks for smoothies.

Use chicken and turkey carcasses to make homemade chicken stock; shells from shellfish and fish bones and skin for seafood stock.

Stock up when things are on sale.

Oatmeal and eggs are cheap. (and good healthy choices)

When fresh fruit is on sale, buy it and freeze it.

Freeze homemade meals in single serving containers. In a baking tray, use aluminum foil to make sections. Put raw chicken in each section. Cook one with a red sauce/mushrooms/onions; the next with lemon and spices; the next a barbecue sauce etc. Most chicken is cooked the same except for the topping. Cook 3-4 meals at one time, and freeze it. It also saves money on oven use (this is also a time saver cook once for many meals).

The journey to a healthy weight is just that....
a journey.

For many of us who struggle to get to that special number, I think comfort comes when you finally realize that there is never a true destination. Yes, there is a goal weight and it is very important to maintain that weight and address gain issues before they are too large to get back into line. Making healthy choices and not falling into some old poor habits is a lifetime process. So, once I truly appreciate the fact that this is for life, then I try to find ways to enjoy the ride. I spend lots of time associating this thinking to a vacation as a child. I can remember asking time after time, "Are we there yet?" I also remember getting bored along the way and venturing off into troubled lands. Like the time, on a car trip from North Carolina to Florida, for my first visit of Disney. Boy, was I ever excited. But, shortly after we began the journey my brother began to pick on me. We were traveling in a car, and then there was not TV to entertain little minds. Before I knew what had happened we were swinging at each other and my mother was shouting. I won't repeat what, but I still remember the tone. You get the idea. After a period of sulking, I remember truly enjoying the car games we had made up and copied from other's ideas. The association from this is that getting to the vacation spot can be just as much fun as the actual vacation. I was sharing this association with a member recently. She looked as if the light came on and said so you start the vacation before you ever leave home. From that point on, her attitude toward weight loss and maintaining a healthy weight changed. She began trying new recipes and foods and sharing those ideas with other people. She has taught me a lot and I have enjoyed trying some of her cultural choices and adding some of those recipes to my favorites. Healthy choices are contagious. Her habits have changed her mother, her adult sister, her husband and her children. The more people you can take with you on this journey the more enjoyable it will be.

Maybe, you received this book as a gift, from someone who cares for you very much. I have a person in mind that I would love to brush over his story. My understanding is that he has been at an unhealthy weight all his teenage and adult life. He had shared many stories about playing sports in high school and college and the benefit of being heavy. He was very physical and considered himself healthy, until an automobile accident caused a terrible back and hip injury that resulted in several months of bed rest. The decreased activity and the habit of taking in a few too many calories and making some high fat and sugar choices resulted in a 75 pound gain. When he was able to bear weight again therapy was long and very difficult. Exasperated by the additional pounds. He did not lose the weight, but was able to go back to work and become a productive person. However those old eating habits were still giving him problems and he continued to gain 12-15 pounds a year. When we met he was desperate and the changes were slow. I always gave him a smile when he described himself as "crock pot". I watched him slowly adopt some of the tips and habits of Living Healthy, Living Well and he is now well on his way to changing his future by reaching a healthy number.

The stories go on and on, I would love to hear from you and learn of the successes you have had. Your journey and tips, trials and successes. You can reach me at Phyllis.Bullins@Beefit.org. I look forward to hearing from you.

If you enjoy the recipes included here, a hard bound cook book, Eating Healthy, Eating Well is available for $15.00 plus $4.95 shipping and handling. Send check made payable to BeeFit PO Box 8049, West Grove, PA 19390. Your new hard bound cook book will be shipped within 48 hours.

Have fun with the process!

Regards,

Phyllis

Thank you first of all to my beautiful family, who has supported me through my weight loss and by vision to educate the public to the simple steps to get to a healthy weight and stay there. To my husband, Mike, who continues to astonish me by his constant dedication to health and fitness. To by beautiful daughter Emilie, who has educated her mother to the advantages of modern day technology, and is responsible for helping to get the art and photographs in this book. And a special thank you to Michael who first taught me that it is hunger to listen to and not fullness. Boy, was that the most valuable lesson I ever learned. I sometimes have to relive the conversation and put it into practice over and over, but that memory and awareness is one of the keys to my continued success.

To all the hundreds of people who have helped me along the way, from words of wisdom to recipes and how to information. I realize that the tools I have for success were shared with love and genuine desire for my success. A huge thank you to everyone that has shaped me to the healthy person I am today.